RISK CAPITAL

A portfolio of financial shenanigans

James Ellman

Seacliff Publications

A graduate of Harvard Business School and a former field agent for the Federal Reserve Bank of New York, the author spent more than 20 years running billions of dollars as a Portfolio Manager of both Mutual Funds and Hedge Funds in New York and San Francisco at firms ranging from Merrill Lynch, to AIM to Ascend Capital. Mr. Ellman resides in Tiburon, CA with his wife and sons.

The growth of the capital markets since the 1990s has handed enormous power to a handful of men and women answerable to no one except their investors. What happens when this power is used for personal greed and ambition? RISK CAPITAL takes you on a global ride from the cool glass towers of Manhattan to the steamy jungles of the Yucatan - from secret meetings in a mountain-top Swiss castle to the very depths of evil men's souls.

Praise for RISK CAPITAL

'Cross the Magellan Fund with James Bond and Gordon Gecko and you've got James Ellman's RISK CAPITAL'

Mike Yellen, Portfolio Manager, AIM Global Health Care Fund

'If it sells a million copies it will be a best seller.'

James Bogin, Founder, Legend Asset Management

'James Ellman is the early 21st Century's answer to Jonathan Swift'

Andrew Boczek, President and Chief Investment Officer, Gulliver Investments LLC

'Long at the top, short at the bottom'

Brian Urey, Emerging Markets Trader, Robert Fleming Securities

Contents

Hedge Shot

Front-Runners

Insider Trading

Time Equals Money

Bear Trap

Tartan Lounge

Smallcap

Knowledge Workers

HEDGE SHOT

George Corinth shorted three million shares of Boeing at $74 and looked up in time to scope out two sets of string bikini tops as they rollerbladed by. George's eyes lingered for a moment across the beach and at the ocean broken by the piers of the Santa Monica Boardwalk before returning his attention to the laptop computer on his thighs. Bloomberg stock quote software flashed across the screen as data raced into the computer. In the middle of the display an active window showed a real time video feed of United Continental Airline's president at a news conference in Chicago as he announced another quarter of disastrous earnings. George's finger still rested on the GO button that had triggered the Boeing stock sale. He moved his hand to his shirt pocket as his cell phone buzzed.

"Corinth."

"Thanks for the trade big guy," said the Oxbridge English accent on the other end of the line. It was Peter Roberts, the salesman from BankAmerica Merrill Lynch who handled the account for Wave InterCapital, George's employer. The number of institutional salesmen with British accents in the U.S. is astounding. Diction may have no bearing on ability, but it certainly helped to woo over the Yanks.

"No problem Pedro. I just thought you could use a new LazyBoy." George unconsciously squinted through the noontime smog to his right. If not for the pollution it might have been possible to actually see the new Roberts estate in Malibu - a structure owing much of its oceanfront view to commissions derived from Wave Intercapital trading activity.

"Don't you worry. I'll make sure there's something soft for you to put your weight down on anytime you want to stop by. Hold on." Someone on the trading floor yelled out for quiet. "Here it comes George."

In a slightly time-delayed stereo from both the phone at his ear and the computer's speaker George was able to hear the voice of United Continental's president.

"So in light of the drop in demand for our services globally, and our current financial losses, we have decided to cancel the budgeted purchase of 85 new aircraft this year, and delay 2018's purchases until 2019 at the earliest."

George's smile was the exact opposite of the CEO's tight frown clearly depicted on the screen below. Boeing stock ticked down to $72.50. Volume on the stock soared. In little cubicles in Manhattan, analysts were pulling up spreadsheets and adjusting down their sales and, thus, earnings for the great American aircraft maker.

"Want to cover now or later, big guy?"

"Oh I think I'll let this one ride for awhile Pedro. I need some lunch. Talk to you after the close." Boeing hit $71.75 as George flipped the phone closed and hauled his 240 pounds of bulk off the bench. As he walked he caught the eye of a young blonde waiting on tables at Raoul's Cafe. Great bod, average face, but certainly good enough for a quick trade. He smiled but she turned away to avoid his attentions, a hint of disgust in her manner.

A flash of quick anger welled up in his chest and tightened his throat. Just three years ago he had been in good shape from working out every day in the gold-plated Shad Hall Gymnasium at Harvard Business School. Now, 35 months at a hedge fund and 60 pounds later he could only get a chick's attention with a roll of bills and his 1980 classic convertible Mercedes. He waited until he was as close as possible, until her turned back was only a few feet away.

"Too bad. If you had a nice smile I might have given you a bit part." She turned and stared. In jeans and a sport shirt, it was hard to tell. Was this guy a real producer, or maybe just a mid-level manager who had been 'right-sized' right out of a job? George's confident and cruel smirk was enough to cut though the blonde's already shaky confidence. He could see the pain in her eyes as he walked on. No one, especially not an underemployed actress hoping for work, should insult a man who received a $7.6 million bonus in 2016 for betting much of his hedge fund's $1.1 billion on the winning side of the Swiss Franc's collapse.

A block and a half later, George arrived at the tall glass box of a building that Wave Intercapital called home. The sun was bright against the tinted panes, but inside the marble atrium the air was cool and gentle. A polite nod from the guard, and a complete lack of response from the obviously superior human with the laptop, and George was in the elevator on his way to the eighth, and top floor.

The doors opened to reveal a stunning view of the ocean stretching out to forever in front of his eyes. The glass of the window reached from ceiling to floor and was not tinted so as to make one squint when emerging from the elevator. George nodded politely, but stiffly, to the attractive brunette behind the great mahogany reception desk and she returned the gesture as he strode past. Elizabeth and George had hooked up a few times a couple of years back, but things had not worked out well (a normal occurrence for both parties).

A security card held against a magnetic panel, and frosted glass doors slid open allowing George to enter the trading floor. This area was completely different from that of the airiness of the lobby due to the perception of cramped space. The floor was higher to allow for cable and wire access. Seating areas were arrayed in a circle with printers, data terminals and even archaic fax machines around the outside. Analysts and traders sat in this area. George nodded to the traders, and sneered slightly at the analysts. The traders, back-office types who had worked their way up through desire and an ability to wake up at 4 a.m., were too busy talking on the phones and entering trade tickets on their computers to make much of a response. However, the analysts, fresh MBAs, looked up eagerly from reading brokerage-published research to acknowledge George's presence. One even waved. It was hard to imagine that just a few years ago George Corinth, net worth $17.9 million, had actually been one of those bootlickers.

Along the walls were the glass-enclosed partners' offices. George occupied the smallest of these. He fell back into the black leather armchair behind his desk which faced away from the window and towards the trading pit before him. His eyes fell to the trading screen. Boeing, $80/$80.25.

George's fist smashed down onto the desk. He could see the message light blinking on his office phone. Certainly, at least one of the blinks represented a message from Simon Carr, Managing Principal, wanting to know how the most junior equity holder in the organization had managed to lose more than $18 million in less than an hour.

"What's up boss?" asked Jack Kinkaid, the new analyst, as he nervously moved into the office.

"What happened to Boeing?" George yelled so loud that the traders in the pit, rarely fazed by anything, turned their heads momentarily toward the glass office.

"Well, first United reported the cutback in orders, and that sent the stock down." George made quick circles of irritation with his hand, "Then China came across the tape saying that they had had a falling out with Airbus and that Boeing was going to supply them with 450 new planes over the next decade, to be built at a new joint venture plant outside of Shanghai."

George glowered at the analyst who was only six weeks out of Stanford Business School. The kid had no brains but was the scion of a family of real estate magnates in Boston. This alone was enough to guarantee him admission to every top 10 B-school in the country. George had hired the kid because he liked having someone with a trust fund doing his errands.

8

After blinking into the Corinth stare for a moment, the greenhorn decided he had better not show weakness by leaving without first stating his reason for entering partner territory without an invitation.

"I really think you should go long Russia. The economy is really chugging along, and the recovery that everyone thinks is so fragile is going to continue at least for the next year. I can show you some of the current account and non-portfolio investment inflow numbers."

"I'll think about it," George grumbled. "Why don't you come back in a couple of hours with your data?"

Kinkaid smiled thankfully and closed the door as he left. George turned his back on the trading pit as he swiveled his chair towards the window and put his feet up on a low bookcase. Hundreds of black scuff marks around his shoes on the wood showed that this was a preferred work position. With no one able to see, his hands clenched the armrests, his throat tightened and his eyes filled with hot tears of anger and the blue of the Pacific Ocean swam before his gaze.

Two years ago had been amazing, as if God had been behind every one of his trades. Not only had he been right on every position, he knew he was right, which made it that much easier to convince the seniors to lever up bets well above what any rational man would have accepted without such assurance. George was the reason that the investment performance of Wave's main fund was 148% in that year against a down U.S. market, and he knew it.

But now, nothing was working. No, it was worse than that: God seemed to be playing against George this year. He had been so right on that Boeing trade, but a damned deus ex machina had been lowered down to rip victory away! It's just not fair, he thought. Just six months ago he had been a big hero, and now the Managing Principal had given him twelve weeks to earn back what he had lost so far this year. Then the Boeing trade - another eighteen in the hole!

9

It also was not fair that his $18 million bucks did not go that far. After buying the big house for three, decorating it, and picking up the Mercedes convertible and the Lotus, and paying taxes, and having so much locked up in firm partnership units, there just was not that much left. George could not bring himself to accept the situation. Why were other people so lucky?

He wiped his eyes with the back of his hand and pulled himself together as he made his decision. He walked out of the office without saying a word and rode the elevator to the garage. Sliding behind the wheel of his convertible, George pulled out a cheap 'burner' cellphone. He dialed a local number and could hear from the connection that there was a cellular phone on the other end."

"Yeah?"

"Corinth."

"We on?"

"Yeah."

"Agreed time and place?"

"Yeah."

"Better get a move on," the line clicked dead leaving George shaking and cold even as he stood in the sunny street.

LAX was a blur of multi-ethnic movement. Cambodian immigrants pushed past visiting Dutch tourists who were themselves trying not to step on the prayer rugs of a group of Muslim businessmen facing towards a 747 that happened to be blocking their view of Mecca. George walked slowly and cautiously through the fray, occasionally looking over his shoulder to make sure that he was not being followed. At the entrance to the coffee shop he could see Diego waiting for him in a booth. George doubted that this was the man's real name, but it was what he had been given. It was obviously best not to ask too many questions in this transaction. At their last meeting the well-groomed Hispanic man had been wearing a beautifully fitted dark blue double breasted suit. Now he was sitting in a red vinyl booth in a loud Hawaiian shirt, drinking an espresso. His client sat down and nodded.

Diego put down his cup and wrapped his hands around its warmth as he spoke, "Well, are we in business?" The accent was certainly Hispanic, but faint.

"I want it done." George's voice was steadier than expected.

"Good...you have the money?" The question was asked in a confident, unrushed manner.

George nodded. "I have already authorized the wire to your Cayman account." As we agreed. Half now, half after you are done.

"Good...You know the time, you know the place. I would advise you to not delay transmission of the second installment upon completion. May you have a healthy life." Diego stood up and left the restaurant without looking back.

George sat in the booth for a few minutes longer. The weight of the act swept over him for a moment, and then it was gone, replaced with a chest-swelling feeling of victory. Once again, George Corinth was going to be a star! He strode happily out of the terminal to the parking area, humming as he went. He gave the eye to every little hotty he passed wondering when he would get his next trade.

Hernan Canterra eased himself into 3A, the leather business class seat of American Airlines Flight 34: LAX-Dallas-Cancun. He looked a bit like Tom Selleck, and the Hawaiian shirt accentuated the resemblance. He turned down the cheap complimentary champagne and procured a large orange juice from the stewardess. Ever since he had gotten drunk and almost slept through a planned hit in 2008, Hernan had cut back on alcohol. Being a hired killer was a strange profession, but one in which a man could learn to take pride in his efficiency and profitability. He had started off harmlessly enough, working as a patriot in the special forces of the government of his native Argentina, but after the Malvinas War, a change of locale became necessary. Working for his friends in Bogota was lucrative, but increasingly constraining. After one spends enough time in the United States, the urge to become an entrepreneur evolves into a necessity. Just as a computer programmer leaves IBM for a start-up, an assassin finds that his talents become more remunerative when one is self-employed.

As usual, Canterra carried no weapon while traveling. He would pick up what he needed for the job as close to the needed time as necessary, and then discard it as soon as possible. While he appreciated hand-crafted firearms, he had no particular love for the instruments of his trade. All of us are born with a compunction against killing. But training (usually in the army, or the streets of a slum) can teach us not to care when we kill. After a while, the death of another to defend a motherland, generate a fee, or eliminate a competitor is of little consequence. Canterra had stopped caring more than fifteen years ago.

The jet landed in Dallas close to midnight without event, and an hour later Canterra was once again airborne and heading for Mexico. While in the last two decades Cancun had become Fort Lauderdale with the Margaritas priced in pesos, the airport still looked very Mexican. The floors were a shiny black, and even in the early morning the humidity was high enough to make one expect an indoor rain shower. Canterra patiently waited in the long line of incoming gringo tourists. They were quickly processed by dour-faced Mayans who stamped passports so many times a day to surely cause repetitive-motion injuries whenever some Norte Americano lawyer got around to the idea. Canterra presented his genuine, if illegally procured, passport and entered the state of Quintana Roo as just another vacationer interested in nothing more than sun, surf and cerveza.

At the Dollar Rent-A-Car outlet a large, air-conditioned Chevrolet was quickly obtained, and Canterra drove onto the main highway. However, at the turn-off for the Zona Hotelera Turistica, the Chevy continued straight and was soon on the Autopista pointed for the colonial city of Merida.

George sidled back into the office at his normal time of 5:30am with an hour to spare before the market opened. The traders and most of the analysts had already been at their desks for an hour or more. The newest partner at Wave Intercapital checked his screens, ordered a jumbo breakfast of eggs, ham and pancakes from the Wave's private chef, and then stepped into the firm's gym to see what sort of a sweat he could build up in 30 minutes. During his first years at the firm, George had sneered at those who worked out when they could have been making money. However, now that he was a partner and had to help pay for the facilities, George found the perq almost a necessity.

After a shower, and the first sip of orange juice at his desk, George picked up his phone and hit the button for Jill Harrison. The trader picked up, and turned to look across the room at George. She was not the type one would have expected to be an experienced short-trader at a hedge fund. In her early 30s, she had been at a trading desk for almost ten years.

"What's up today big boy?"

George replied through a mouthful of scrambled eggs, "I want to short Mexico."

"Stocks? The peso?"

"All of it. I want options on the currency, I want puts on the Bolsa Index, and if you can short some Cetes, I'll take that too."

A bit of emotion entered her voice. A little fear, a little excitement. "How much exposure are we talking about here?"

"My limit is one bill, leveraged ten to one. Morgan will extend the funds, and probably take a lot of our action as well."

"One billion dollars?"

"Yeah, I wasn't speaking Spanish, was I?"

"No, but I'll have to clear this with Carr."

"That's fine Harrison. And don't worry about paying the interest on the borrowed funds, this trade shouldn't take too long."

"O.K., I will get back to you in a bit, I'll be busy getting this done."

"Fine, my ham is getting cold." George put the phone down and began to focus his monitors to bring him more detailed info on the state of the Mexican markets. Not that he did not already know. He had been planning for this day.

La Ciudad Blanca, the White City of Merida, dawned clear and warm. Breezes blowing south from the Gulf of Mexico hinted at the heat and humidity of the day to come. Canterra strolled out of the Merida Mission Hotel dressed as a Catholic priest in a long flowing cloak which made him appear a bit heavier than his true lean self. He smiled at the mass of people passing him on the street: young school children in uniforms, old men in fedoras, young women in office outfits, gringos studying at the University of the Yucatan. Canterra strode calmly past a number of local police and Federales as he entered the Plaza de la Independencia.

A killer dressed as a priest, one of the oldest tricks, but still effective. In less than two minutes he reached the great fortress-like Merida cathedral. The church was built on the site of, as well as from the stones of, a pre-conquest Mayan temple. It dominated the other impressive buildings flanking the square. After passing the multiple indigent at the door, the interior sanctuary was starkly plain for a Mexican house of God. Canterra took the back stairway to an access door, and then climbed ten final meters up a fire escape ladder to the roof. By lying near the edge, he was invisible to those below despite his excellent view of the entire Plaza. Now he had only to wait.

Jill Harrison was in an awkward spot. Shorting a billion dollars' worth of Mexican securities was not the easiest thing to do quickly. Liquidity always seemed to dry up just when it was needed most. She had received a second call from that fat slob Corinth and had been told to complete the position by 10am - no excuses. As if that did not already represent enough pressure, Carr had actually come out of his office to speak to her in person, instead of on the phone, something he rarely did. The analysts tried to look like they were still working when the Managing Principal reached the trading desks, but their silence belied their motive: they were trying to hear what Carr had to say.

"I can't believe this crap!" he growled, looking through the glass partition at George Corinth in his office. George had his back to the door and was facing the ocean.

"Don't blame me boss, I just follow orders," relied Harrison.

"Great excuse. Just remember, at these levels Corinth has a razor thin stop-loss. If he hits that limit, do not hesitate. Unwind those positions immediately! Understood?"

The trader detached one of two phones from an ear so as to look interested as she replied with a bit of sarcasm, "Yes sir, big boss sir."

Carr grunted in disgust and walked into Corinth's office without knocking. George swiveled his chair around to face his superior in silence keeping his eyes averted toward the floor. Carr waited a moment, jaw muscles clenched, put his hands into the pockets of his perfectly tailored Brooks Brothers suit, and decided to break the silence first. As he did, George smiled ever so slightly in the knowledge that he was supposed to grovel and to have spoken first.

"What the hell are you up to? I am just about to meet with those Bechtel people about getting them to keep their account with us, and now I hear you are running up a billion dollar short position in a market that has been red hot all year. I do not need crap like this today. Do you hear me?"

"Mexico will go down today," George replied quietly.

"Nothing else brass balls? Any analysis backing up a bet on this much of the firm's money."

"No."

"Understand me, if you lose one basis point too many, I am closing you down. I will not pour one hundred million dollars of the firm's capital down the drain for the hunch of my most junior partner who has gone cold, not to mention soft, on me."

George just shrugged.

"I better not get called out of this meeting to clean up your mess." Carr turned on his Bally wing tipped heel and strode swiftly out of the office. After a couple of moments, Kinkaid crept in. George had tuned in a Mexican television channel off the satellite and was staring at the screen with the sound off.

"Morning, boss."

16

"I'm pretty busy right now, Kinkaid."

"I just wanted to know why you are putting such a position on in such a hurry?"

"Mexico is going down today," was the flat answer. Kinkaid tensed to ask another question, thought better of it, and crept out of the office making sure to close the door behind him. After consulting with the other three analysts, each picked up a phone and placed orders for their respective personal accounts. All of them bought Mexican securities long, except Kinkaid, who shorted them. He was the only one who had taken the time to look into George Corinth's eyes.

Security was now in place, the bunting had been hung, and it was time for the inauguration of the new Governor of the State of Yucatan, Jose' Chetumal. It was a big day for the ruling PRI party. Not only was Chetumal the PRI candidate, but his appearance clearly indicated Mayan decent. Merida was only a few hour's drive from Chiapas where peasant Zapatistas simmered on the edge of rebellion. The PRI victory was hailed by many as a reaffirmation of the party's legitimacy, and right to resume its long rule.

Hernan Canterra had long-ago finished assembling the high powered hunting rifle whose components had been hidden under his robes and was scanning the crowd for his target. He made sure to keep the end of the barrel from pointing over the roof edge so as to remain unseen. The telescopic sight brought everything close enough. He caught sight of Chetumal shaking hands in the crowd. Suddenly, the target came into sight: Ernique Frijoles, President of the Republic of Mexico, surrounded by his bodyguards. Once reviled and accused of incompetence as he took office, Frijoles now enjoyed wide popularity. The economy was growing again, the PRI had done well in recent local elections, and Nafta-related benefits were apparent in continued industrialization.

As the President ascended the podium, Canterra took aim. Shots to the body were out. One never knew who might be wearing a Kevlar vest these days.

On the television window on his computer screen, George watched Mexican news commentators in the crowd in Merida yacking away silently with the sound muted. A recently-made lunch of rare swordfish steak and garlic French fries on his desk was ignored. The President appeared on the podium. He smiled to the cameras. Then his head was no longer there. There was a burst of bright red and the body disappeared from view under an avalanche of security guards.

Canterra was running before Zedillo's body hit the stage. He had been in his line of work long enough to know when a shot hit home. He shimmied down the fire-escape ladder, and took most of the interior steps two at a time, brushing dust off his robes as he moved. His gait slowed to a confident walk for the last flight as he came into view of the pulpit, and then he walked out the door into a raging confusion. More than one person was screaming, sirens could already be heard, and while many in the square were running for cover, the other half seemed to be in a daze. A cordon of police was forming to seal off the plaza. Just as a Federale raised his hand to stop Canterra from leaving, the bomb went off. Not only did it blow much of the roof off the Cathedral and destroy the evidence of the rifle, the plastique charge also did a wonderful job of distracting the attention of the police. The killer strode down Calle 59 as a man of God, and ten minutes later was once again a Hawaiian shirt-wearing gringo tourist in a Chevy heading down the road to the sun and fun of Cancun.

Within seconds of that one high-caliber shot, all the traders' phones at Wave Intercapital lit up with calls from salesmen hoping to be the first to convey the deadly news and generate a quick trade. For a moment the three traders could do nothing but try to field the barrage of calls but as the news sunk in, they put their receivers down and looked towards George Corinth's office. He had turned his back on the trading floor and was facing the ocean with his feet up and his lunch plate in his lap. All his trading screens of Mexican securities were glowing red, the color of falling prices. George stared out at the waves and took the first bite of his lunch. It was the best swordfish he had ever tasted.

FRONT-RUNNERS

The snow was falling steadily at 7:54AM on Thursday morning as the delayed 6:00AM shuttle landed at Boston's Logan airport. To Louisa Jacobson, the downtown skyline was just a blur as she leaned her forehead against the little round window. The cold plastic helped to wake her up and clear out the cobwebs. It had already been a long morning and she knew she needed a pick-me-up as soon as possible. The lights were too bright and the air too stale for her and the sense of claustrophobia was constant. Making things even worse was the constant pressure against her side of the bulky form of Enrique Tinoco, President of Panama's Banco del Exterior. She could tell that he was leering at her legs, and that in his mind's eye her dark blue skirt had been removed long ago.

The 737 taxied to the gate and the usual mad rush of Type-A people who commuted on the overpriced New York/Boston flight grabbed their briefcases and vibrated in place as they waited for the banker/lawyer/consultant/salesman directly in front of them to move. Louisa's card stated that she was a member of the Emerging Market division of Silverman, Satchel, & Co's Corporate Finance Department. Technically a banker, her usual activities placed her much more in the range of sales - there was always another deal to pitch, there was always competition, and Silverman, Satchel always got its share. Thus the firm guaranteed a high ranking in the league tables, not to mention massive payouts for the partners and managing directors.

Today her job was clearly one of sales, and a most distasteful one at that: Silverman, Satchel was the lead investment bank running the books for the government privatization of Banco del Exterior and it was the last day of the roadshow to try and drum up U.S. investors dumb enough to buy the deal. Panama had finally come around to the University of Chicago mantra for economic growth of tight

20

money, competition, and open markets. Thus, the government had decided to sell 65% of its largest commercial bank in an attempt to raise some much needed cash as well as to show the world that it was serious about reform.

Banco del Exterior specialized in the sort of private banking encouraged by Panama's stringent financial secrecy laws - massive accounts tied to narcotics barons, arms peddlers and tinpot dictators' rainy day coup funds. The bank was extremely profitable because while its customers demanded that no questions be asked, they were usually not particularly concerned with the interest rate on their accounts. It was a particularly dirty business, but no worse really than strip mining in Chile, tobacco retailing in the U.S., or the Massachusetts Lottery.

Thus, Louisa found herself crammed in the aisle of the early shuttle between Ernrique Tinoco, and Carlos Ramirez, Banco del Exterior's Chief Financial Officer. After five grueling days in L.A., San Francisco, Denver, Minneapolis, Chicago, and New York, the roadshow was finally coming to an end in Boston. The snow-delayed flight had already put the entourage behind schedule.

As they emerged from the jetway, Dave Salzinger, one of Silverman, Satchel's institutional salesman in Boston was waiting. Corporate Finance tried to pick the best looking graduates of the top business schools, but in sales there was little need for anything but tenacity. If the markets ever took a real dive, most of Silverman's salesmen would happily find themselves selling dog food or condos within a week. Dave was a good example of this. His face was pockmarked, and his beer-gut strained the buttons of his shirt. He was not standard Silverman material, but the intensity of his gaze betrayed his ability to sell anything to anyone.

"Good morning, gentlemen," he boomed to the Panamanians. "Nice day for flying." He nodded towards Louisa who returned the gesture. Before Tinoco or Ramirez could reply, Dave was booming again. "We gotta move guys. We have Mass Financial in 25 minutes, Putnam at 9:30, MFS at 11:00, and then Veracity after lunch. The Panamanians groaned even though they had seen the schedule days in advance, and the entourage shoved off towards the exit. A white stretch limousine was waiting at the curb and the four piled in.

Steve chattered amiably as he pointed out his favorite Italian restaurants of East Boston, and the usually talkative Panamanians nodded quietly as they saved their voices for the day ahead. Finally, Ramirez spoke as yet another Dunkin' Donuts shop hove into view. "I don't care if we are late, but I need to get some coffee." Dave raised an eyebrow but motioned to the driver to pull over.

"Who wants one? We have to move here," Dave bellowed. Tinoco and Louisa shook their heads and Ramirez and the salesman rushed in. Tinoco's hand stretched out and began to squeeze Louisa's upper thigh. She smiled at him and met his eyes. He was not all that bad looking for his age, and he seemed to understand the way the game worked.

"Not now Enrique," she said almost playfully. "I'll see you in a moment, I'm going to go use the bathroom." She felt horribly tight inside.

Her hand hit the door handle and she was out. The cold snow swarmed into her eyes and made them water. The wind blew her blond hair in all directions. She made it into the store and headed for the bathroom. Locking the one stall door behind her, Louisa fished a wooden bullet shaped container on a string out from under her blouse. A half turn and its top was open. Exhaling first, she took two long hard snorts of coke and leaned against the gray metal partition wall. The effect was almost instantaneous. The tension floated away, her teeth became numb, her energy flowed, Louisa Jacobson was her true self once more.

The limo pulled up in front of the graceful arched structure of the Rowe's Wharf Building, Veracity Investments' new headquarters at 1:00PM. The entourage was rested and ready after lunch, and right on time for the meeting - after all one did not want to be late for a chance to pitch an investment to the world's largest active asset managers.

Salzinger breezed his charges past security, clearly a regular to the building, and the elevator whisked them up to the top floor. The reception atrium was light and airy despite the pallor of the wintry sky outside, and the slate gray of the ocean appeared as a giant cold, heaving beast through the giant windows. The visitors were immediately escorted into one of the two glass-enclosed conference rooms flanking the receptionist's desk. Salzinger began to pump himself up for the inevitable hand shaking and introductions. The Panamanians singed their raw throats with hot tea and ran once again through their notes even though there was rarely a new question this late in a roadshow. Louisa simply settled into a corner and tried to relax: she would only need to step in if there was a problem.

The Veracity people showed up suddenly and all at once. There was Sue O'Connor, the head of Latin American Investments, Joseph Paris, the regional banking analyst, and Gregory Cohn, an emerging markets specialist. Outwardly they were calm and friendly, but their eyes were hard and one could see from their movements that the pressure to perform had them wound up tight. Veracity was well known for ejecting underperforming investment managers onto the cold harsh pavement with little notice. From there a Veracity alum often had to settle for lesser employment at one of the large insurance companies or Swiss banks whose fund management businesses always seemed to trail behind those of the entrepreneurial independents.

Louisa sat patiently through most of the presentation, listening yet again to bull points for buying the soon to be issued ADRs of Banco del Exterior: regional GDP growth, strict banking secrecy, growing consumer borrowing demand, full privatization, and management's 20% share ownership incenting a rising return on equity. Finally she had to leave the room when the Q&A began with the same questions that she had heard at every other roadshow presentation. A couple of quick snorts in the bathroom, and she was back under control.

As Louisa was returning to the reception area, she saw her boyfriend, Dan Lee, coming out of the elevator. They had hoped to bump into each other here. Dan was one of Silverman Satchel's analysts for the biotech industry and was scheduled to meet with the portfolio manager of Veracity's Select Health Care Fund. Louisa liked him because of his attractive looks, Stanford Business School pedigree, and ability to get his hands on lots of very high grade coke.

"Hey big guy," she said in way of greeting.

"Always a pleasure to see one of our friends from corporate finance," he replied. As he approached they shook hands, and his free left hand came up and squeezed her right arm just a little too long. Louisa could feel herself growing warmer.

"How's business?" she asked quietly.

"Lousy," he replied in kind. "The whole biotech group is going down the drain and everyone knows it. It really sucks because we have done so many deals in the last year that I can't get too negative and put a Sell on most of the stocks in the sector. How about you?"

"All right since I can see the light at the end of the tunnel. One more day and the Panamanians will be heading back to their Laundromat."

"Oh come on Lulu. You're just jealous of their customers."

"Hey look Dan, that's Oscar Mellon."

Dan turned around casually, and sure enough, there was Oscar Mellon, lead Portfolio Manager of the Columbus Fund - the largest active mutual fund in the world with assets of almost $175 billion. The two investment bankers nodded respectfully to the walking market mover who smiled back kindly to these two people whom he had never met.

As he got to the desk the receptionist looked up, "Here's your package Oscar. Your daughter dropped it off a few moments ago while you were meeting with the President. It looks like a present." Oscar took the brightly wrapped box from her hand and chuckled.

"Yup, well it's my birthday"

"She's darling. How old is little Lisa now?"

"Thirteen."

"And how old are you now birthday boy?"

"Sorry Linda, that's classified."

Oscar was shaking the package gently as he walked back past Dan and Louisa.

"What do you think it is?" Louisa asked. Oscar looked up and seemed to actually see them as people for the first time, and not just as another couple of the hundreds of faceless investment bankers who hounded after Veracity's money every market day of the year.

"Well, I think it might be an ant farm. My daughter doesn't like my working so much. She claims that we are all like ants in these glass buildings here in downtown. She wants me to buy a ranch so she can become a cowboy, or cowgirl, or something like that."

"Well, happy birthday sir," Dan offered.

"Thank you. I will. Take care now." Oscar turned a corner and disappeared back into the warrens of Veracity.

"I gotta go Dan. I better get back to the dog and pony show."

"See you tonight? My place, at nine?" Louisa nodded her assent, let out a wicked little smile, turned and reentered the conference room just in time to hear Tinoco deny for the umpteenth time in the last week that Banco del Exterior had absolutely no drug money in any of its deposit accounts.

The weather-delayed the 5PM shuttle so that it did not touch down at LaGuardia until half past seven. Tinoco wanted Louisa to come back to his hotel room, but she begged off having to take care of work at home that had piled up on her desk over the last couple of days. The limo dropped her off at Dan's place at 80th and Lexington. The snow had turned to rain as it usually did when one crossed into Manhattan: the heat given off by all the tension, idling taxi engines, fired up crack pipes, burning garbage and open steam vents was usually enough to defeat any snowflake.

Louisa nodded to Alfredo, the doorman, as she walked through the building's lobby on the way to the elevators. The car whisked her quickly up to the thirty-second floor. The door open instantly when she knocked - Alfredo had given her away again. Dan grabbed her around the waist, slammed the door, and was kissing her and ripping off her blouse and unzipping her skirt before she could even drop her purse and briefcase to the floor. As he unbuckled his jeans she pushed past him and found several lines of coke and a rolled up hundred dollar bill waiting for her on a mirror placed horizontally on his bed. Louisa paused briefly and came up for air as Dan turned down the lights behind her. She looked outside the window at the falling rain and the lights of the rushing cars on the FDR Drive and the slower moving ships on the East River suddenly jumped into insane clarity.

Dan left at 5AM the next morning, and Louisa luxuriated for an hour in his bed. She had never been all that partial to his extra-hard futon, but anything felt better than an airline seat to someone who had logged more than 200,000 airmiles in the last year. Finally, she forced herself into the shower and dressed for work. She walked out onto the street to confront an absurdly beautiful day for January in New York. The huge radio-dispatched Town Car from Silverman was waiting for her. The driver, a lurking sort of guy, was wearing all black.

"How are you this morning?" he asked in a heavy Russian accent. She held up a hand over her forehead to block the glare and to try and get a look at his eyes through the rear view mirror. A beam of pure whiteness flashed onto her face, and sent a stab of pain deep into her brain.

"Give me your shades," she ordered.

"I don't want to sell them Ms. Jacobson," he said reading her name off of his dispatch order. "They fit my head too good."

"Ok, I'll rent them just for the drive downtown."

"How much?"

"40 bucks."

The driver shrugged and handed over the sunglasses. Louisa gave him two new twenties.

"You know, lady. People work for a whole day in a coal mine in Russia for $40."

"Sucks for them," she said coldly. The driver looked back at her through his window for a moment. He said nothing else for the rest of the drive.

Silverman Satchel's headquarters was a big, solid and ugly building on Sixth Avenue near enough to Times Square to make the neighborhood uncomfortable. It had been thrown up in the last great burst of building as the 2002-2007 binge came to an end. Opulent sculpture, fountains, floral arrangements and marble greeted Louisa as she entered the lobby. The guards knew her well, there were not that many blondes built like her in the whole City, still they checked her ID badge.

The Emerging Market Finance department, a sprawling empire, covered almost three floors of the building. Louisa had hardly had a chance sit down in her small office and start looking over her e-mails when a lawyer she had never seen before walked in without knocking. She knew he was a lawyer by his imperious bearing, white collar and cuffs on blue shirt, yellow tie and red silk pocket square. It was not that none of the investment bankers dressed as loudly, but that the lawyers somehow carried themselves and looked a bit different. The thought of being from a cost center department whose primary job was to say 'no' to the profit centers made Louisa's face pucker up in the same way as the permanent look on her visitor's countenance.

"Mr. Sinclair would like to see you."

Louisa knew she was in trouble, but had no idea as to why - had something gone wrong with the Banco del Exterior deal? Sinclair was the head of Latin American Corporate Finance, and it was not pleasant to see him mad.

When she arrived at Sinclair's corner office, her boss's lean face was even redder than usual as it strained to be free of an overly tight collar of a starched custom dress shirt.

"Please sit down Ms. Jacobson," he ordered. Louisa knew that this was very serious trouble as Sinclair usually referred to her by first name.

The lawyer closed the door and began, "It has come to our attention that you have a chemical dependency problem."

"Who the hell told you that?" Louisa barked in a sudden flash of anger.

"That's not important right now Louisa," Sinclair interjected. "What is important is that such behavior cannot be condoned by Silverman, Satchel. We are willing to provide you with a severance payment if you wish to move on, or send you to a top clinic where you can get some help with-"

"I don't have a drug problem!"

"Are you willing to submit to a blood test at this time as stipulated in your employment agreement?" asked the lawyer.

"Screw you all," Lousia said with venom as she swiftly got up and walked out the door. She stopped at her desk only long enough to grab her purse, and then headed for the elevators. The lawyer followed her the entire way, reached into his pocket and brought out a business card which he offered to her.

"I really am sorry about all this. Please give me a call when you have decided what you would like to do." Louisa glared at him. However, her resolve weakened. And just as the elevator opened, she grabbed the card from his grasp. He rode down with her to street level and did not attempt to say anything else.

The air of New York felt and smelled surprisingly clean as Louisa walked through the doors. She was furious, but also relieved in a way. For the last few years she had driven herself hard . The job's pace made her want coke, and the money had kept her habit well stoked. Now she realized that she just wanted to get away. Then her anger returned as she wondered who had turned her in to the management. Could it be Dan? It had better not be.

"Hello," Dan answered his phone at home. Louisa had tried him at work, but his voice-mail answered there.

"What are you doing at home?"

"Collecting unemployment I guess. I got canned this morning. They say I have a drug problem."

"Well, I guess you weren't the asshole who turned me in. They just kicked me out of the building a few moments ago."

"Did you take the settlement?"

"What did they offer you Dan?"

"$800,000 to go away and never come back. If you get the same, what do you say we go to Rio and blow it all? We can be there in time for Carnival. You even said that they have great coke there."

"I'm not going to Rio unless we have a lot more than our settlement offer. I don't know about you, but I don't plan to blow my stake, and come back here to work in some Starbucks dying for a toot."

"So what do you suggest?"

"Stay there Dan. I'll be right over. I have an idea you just might like, as long as you don't mind breaking the law a bit."

"I break the law every day."

Louisa wanted to make some calls to other Silverman workers to find out who had been the rat. Dan had other ideas. He seemed simply happy to be out from under the responsibility of having a job. The couple spent the weekend jumping from one party and nightclub to another. They consumed an entire eight-ball in two days and survived with only a few hours of sleep.

On Monday morning they took a cab directly from the a late night club to Silverman's legal department where the papers were ready to be signed. The presiding lawyer tried to remain stoic, but his yuppie countenance betrayed the disgust he felt for the two ex-bankers. Dan was oblivious, and was only concerned with the signatures and getting the severance check. Louisa was furious about such treatment, but as she rubbed her red-rimmed eyes, and looked over at her boyfriend who was trying to control a sudden nosebleed it suddenly became apparent how pathetic they must have appeared.

"He was a total condescending prick!" she muttered in the cab taking them back uptown. "We made a lot of money for the firm."

"Yeah, but they will just get another couple of b-school drones to take our place. Look, we just got a nice chunk of change. We're free, and we have your plan to make that nest egg grow many times over by Carnival."

"O.k., you're right. But we need to clean ourselves up. He looked at us like we were homeless scum lying in the gutter."

"Screw him Lulu. We'll make it big, and he'll still be some little bootlicker."

On Tuesday, after twenty hours of sleep, they stopped by the Banco del Exterior branch on 59th Street across from Bloomingdale's. With the use of a pen, a fax, and the local manager, the two were able to quickly open an offshore, numbered trading account just like any other drug baron or arms merchant. They spoke on the phone with their new account manager located in Panama City, and told him that they would be wanting to trade US stocks and options as soon as the Silverman checks cleared. They were assured that in two business days the funds would be transferred, and all they needed to do was wait.

On Wednesday they were in Boston. They rented a car at Logan and drove to the upscale suburb of Weston where they were able to use a prepaid master card and an assumed name to rent a small house belonging to a couple of out-of-town snowbirds. Buying a gun in Massachusetts turned out to be extremely difficult, so Dan procured a mean-looking air powered pellet pistol that might at least take out an eye at close range. After that it was just too easy.

Silverman's database had kindly yielded the exact address and phone number in Weston of Oscar Mellon's massive Victorian home on its twelve expansive acres of woods, shrubbery and lawn. On Thursday afternoon at 2:30PM, Mrs. Mellon drove off in her Lexus. At 4:00PM the Weston Public School Bus dropped Lisa Mellon off at the curb, and trundled on down Route 30. Dan drove the car right up the driveway to within a few feet of Lisa before she even turned to see who it was. A quick wave of a gun, a few sharp words, and the thirteen year old Ms. Mellon had joined the two young cokeheads for a ride. Lisa was scared, but quiet, and was soon tied to a chair in the little rented house. They then called their account manager at Banco del Exterior in Panama City and placed trading orders for the next day.

Louisa phoned the Mellon's residence at 6:20PM. Oscar answered the phone.

"Hi. Do you know where your daughter is?"

"She's probably is at a friend's house and will be home soon for dinner," he answered.

"That's not where she is Oscar. You see, we have her here. And we will kill her if we don't get what we want - fast." Lousia held the receiver up to Lisa's mouth as Dan pulled down the gag. Lisa was more than willing to oblige by pleading, "Daddy, I want to go home," in a truly pathetic heartbreaking little voice. For just a moment on the other side of the line there was a pause, and when the portfolio manager spoke again, it was clear that Louisa had his undivided attention.

"Do not hurt her! I will do whatever you ask."

"Good. I want you to write something down. Do you have a pen and paper there?"

"Of course," he replied with anger in his voice.

"Good. Starting at noon tomorrow, you are going to buy the following stocks: Imnex, Bioputer, Enxime, and DNAction. You will buy these stocks until their prices are at least 40% above where you began to buy them. You have until the market closes at 4:00PM to make this happen. If you fail, we will kill darling little Lisa. Do you have all that?"

"Yes...Can't I just pay you money? I have lots. I can get it for you first thing in the morning, and then we can make an exchange-"

"No," Louisa cut him off. "Do it our way, or your daughter is a corpse. Do we have an agreement?"

"Yes."

"Good. We will call you only one more time at this number. And that will be after the market has closed to tell you where Lisa is. It is up to you whether you pick her up dead or alive. I don't think I have to warn you not to call the police, do I?"

"No."

Louisa hung up the phone, and gave Dan a high-five.

Oscar Mellon arrived at work at his normal time of 6:00AM. He left the Mercedes in his assigned underground parking space and took the dedicated Veracity elevator up to his floor. He barely noticed the events around him and was operating almost completely on reflex. Oscar's mind was consumed by thoughts and fears for his daughter. Her life had been as pleasant and fulfilling as possible so far, and now it had been reduced to this - some crappy crime.

Oscar closed the door behind himself upon entering his office, immersed himself in information on stocks, markets and bonds, and tried to make the morning go by. He placed the tickers for the four biotech stocks on his trading screen: IMNX, BIOU, XIME, and DNAN. As the market opened each traded up about a point. A little chat with the trading desk confirmed his suspicion - someone was buying the publicly traded options for the stocks.

At noon, Oscar picked up the phone and called Greg Spandau, his OTC trader.

"Greg, I have some orders for you, I just sent you an e-mail. Open it up." There was a pause as the trader switched applications on his PC. Then a whistle as he read his instructions.

"Oscar, you do realize that these are illiquid stocks with relatively small market caps?"

"Yeah, I know. I expect these orders to be completed in the next two hours."

"What? I can't do that. The stocks will jump in price, we'll have to file reports with the SEC when you hit ownership limits, there will be speculation all over the media about what we are doing."

"I'm not asking for your opinion. Just do it now!" Oscar hung up the phone. Greg looked at his receiver for a moment. If there was one thing that Oscar Mellon was known for besides amazing stock performance, it was politeness. This was just plain weird. But there was no doubt about it, whomever owned these stocks was going to make some money. After a moment's deliberation, he dialed the number of his favorite second cousin, once removed, at his office in San Jose.

34

"Hey Joe. How's it hanging?"

"Fine, but I'm kind of under the gun right now. Can we chat later? Look, you have ten minutes to buy XIME, and DNAN. Do it very fast. Talk to you later."

Greg knew that right now Joe would be sending two trade requests through the internet to E*Trade, and that the on-line discount brokerage firm's computerized system would process the trades within seconds. This was about as safe a way as Greg could devise to make money off Veracity Portfolio Managers' trading activities. Joe's last name was Mucci, and it was unlikely that the SEC would ever trace Greg's familial relationship nor the upside of using E*Trade in Silicon Valley where high-tech company employees were always making shoot-from-the-hip trades in volatile stocks. A few additional trades of a few thousand shares a month would never be noticed. Joe made sure to never actually transfer any traceable monetary assets to Greg, but a new, fully-loaded Isuzu Rodeo 4X4 sat in the garage under the Veracity building.

Greg picked up his phone with the recorded line and pushed the speed-dial button for the trading desk at Silverman, Satchel. His counterpart answered on the other line and orders were placed for IMNX and BIOU. Greg then called Morgan, and more orders went out. As these first two stocks started to rise, he then called the two firms back and put in orders for XIME and DNAN. Finally, he picked up the phone and called Veracity's legal department and asked for the Chief Compliance Officer.

Gail Renolds, CEO of Veracity Investments exuded nothing if not an image of strength. Of course that only made sense considering that the value of her stock in the privately owned company was estimated at more than five billion dollars. Her family controlled additional shares worth another five billion. She was also not just some wall-flower at the company. While her late father, Edward had built the successful firm into its current monstrous size, she had acted as a top performing portfolio manager for almost ten years. Running the company instead of investing in stocks was not as much fun, but everyone had to grow up sometime. She was going over proposals for a new fund statement mailing center when her secretary tapped on the glass of her office door. She waved Jon in. He was very cute, an ex-model, and at thirty about ten years her junior. Ah...the prerogatives of power.

"Lynn from Legal is on line four for you. She says that it is urgent."

"Thanks Jon. I like the tie." Jon looked down at the brightly colored silk, and smiled as he left, closing the door behind him.

Gail hit the speaker phone. "Yes Lynn. What can I do for you?"

"Gail. We have a bit of a problem here. It seems that Oscar Mellon is buying up about twenty percent of four small biotech companies. He has given orders to the trading desk to complete the orders in the next two hours and has indicated that he wants the trades done at any price. As you might imagine, the stocks are going through the roof and I expect the SEC is going to want to talk to us by the end of the day. If nothing else, we will have to file benevolent ownership forms. In addition, the name of such an aggressive buyer will get out to the press, and they will be asking for statements by then end of the day. How should we play this?"

"O.K. Lynn. Don't worry. I'll go talk to Oscar, you just deal with the SEC. Tell them we of course have no intention of making bids for the companies. And just tell the press, 'no comment'."

"Very good Gail. Speak to you later."

'Strange', thought Gail. Oscar was not the type to push stocks around like this. In fact, he rarely bought small hi-tech companies. She got up from her desk and started walking down the hall towards Mellon's office. They knew each other well, as Oscar had been her mentor for years when she ran Veracity's High Growth Fund. Her investment style had eventually become more aggressive than his, but she had to admit that much of what she knew, she had learned from him. He was in his office when she arrived, and she entered without knocking, as he would have done at hers.

"Hi Oscar," she began, taking the seat in front of his cluttered desk. He looked unusually pale.

"Hi Gail. What can I do for you?" He was nervous and unhappy. Something was definitely up.

"You know very well old man," (he was only eight years her senior). "What's up with these biotech stocks? You trying to make some friends over at Harvard Med rich or something?"

"I just want to buy them."

"Why? Why the hurry?"

"Look. I've never had to give you a reason before. My performance is fine this year. Can we just talk about it tomorrow? Let me take these positions, and then we can have a nice long chat." He was scared of something! Gail had never seen him like this before.

"O.K. Oscar. We'll talk later." She got up and left his office. Returning to her own, Gail sat down at her computer and tried to do some research on these four little biotech stocks. In just a few moments she identified a common characteristic: they were unusual in the sector in that they all had listed options. This was starting to get interesting. Time to find out who had been buying up the options earlier in the morning.

Dan and Louisa were ecstatic. The value of their off-shore account had been margined out and completely invested in options of the four biotech stocks that had skyrocked as the underlying shares moved up with Veracity's buying. Mellon had been good to his word, pushing the price of each of his charges up at least 50%. A quick call down to Panama and their holdings were sold and their massive gains harvested. All that was required now was to go and enjoy the loot.

They left Lisa Mellon tied up and in a chair in the nice little rented house and drove the rental to the airport. They checked in for a 5:00PM flight to Dulles with a connection to Panama City. They checked their bags through and proceeded to the gate and waited to board. Dan slid his hand over Louisa's knee as they sat down. She turned her head to whisper in his ear.

"You know, Panama is not that bad a place, and I'm friends with the CEO of Banco del Exterior. I bet he can find us a good investment or two. Maybe after Carnival we can buy up a little government monopoly or something."

"Sounds fine to me Lulu," Dan was just savoring the moment. Clearly he was happy to be out of the investment banking rat race. He was also happy to suddenly be so rich. He chuckled as he recalled that one of his last professional acts at Silverman, Satchel had been to upgrade Imnex and Enxime to 'Buy' status.

The CNN 'Airport Edition' television in the corner of the waiting area finished a story on the Amsterdam Flower Show and moved on to the day's financial news. One of the top stories concerned the unusual trading activities in four biotech stocks and how it was rumored that Veracity was on the point of taking over the companies. The entire biotech sector had traded up on the rumors in expectation that some significant news would soon be released.

"We're the news baby!" Dan whispered in Louisa's ear. She smiled as it was announced that the first class cabin could board the plane. First class for now on, she thought.

The flight to D.C. was uneventful. As the flight for Panama was about to board, Louisa walked over to a payphone and dialed the Mellon's home. Mrs. Mellon picked up the phone, and asked 'hello' in a shaky voice.

"Don't worry," Louisa replied. "Your daughter is just fine. You will find her on 1440 Oak Street. Did you get that?"

"Yes. 1440 Oak."

"Good." Louisa hung up the phone, and got on the plane for Panama.

Panama City dawned warm and hazy. Dan and Louisa slept late, breakfasted at their hotel and caught a taxi down to the main Banco del Exterior branch at 10:00AM. Mr. Rojo, their account officer was expecting them when they arrived at the Private Banking reception area. He was paunchy and old, but well-dressed and distinguished looking nevertheless. Just the sort of person you would want looking over your cash.

"Good mornings Ms. Jacobson, Mr. Lee. Would you please accompany me back to my office?"

"Of course", Louisa replied as he escorted them down a hallway. "We are here to make a partial withdrawal on our account, and we will need an additional wire transfer to a correspondent bank in Rio."

"Yes, yes. We will be happy to assist you both in whatever you may require. Ah, yes. Right here." He held open a door for them.

Dan and Louisa passed through into a large office where they were suddenly grabbed by large security guards, frisked, and forced to sit down in chairs in front of a large desk.

"What the hell?" Dan protested as burly arms held him down.

"I demand to see the President!" Louisa yelled at Rojo.

"The President will be here immediately," he replied. Louisa did not know who to glower at more, Rojo, or the five security men. Then the door opened and Gail Reynolds, Oscar Mellon and three other men entered through a side door. Reynolds took the seat behind the desk. Louisa felt a tightness in her abdomen. Dan's jaw was slack.

"Ms. Jacobson, Mr. Lee," began one of the men who had just entered the room. I am Jaime Gonzolez, Superintendent of the Panamanian Banking Commission. You may be interested to note that late yesterday afternoon, a certain Veracity Investments purchased 51% of the outstanding shares of Banco del Exterior. At the request of Mr. Mellon, the representative of Veracity Investments, a special shareholder meeting was convened early this morning, and Ms. Gail Renolds here was elected President and Chairman of the Board."

There was silence in the room for a moment. Then Renolds smiled and began, "There appears to be a problem with your account. It also appears that," she indicated the two other men who had arrived with her, "Mr. Daily of the SEC, and Mr. Johnson of the FBI would like to ask you two some questions."

"If you don't mind Mr. Gonzolez, we would be more comfortable if we could ask Mr. Lee and Ms. Jacobson those questions back in New York?" asked Johnson. "There is a certain young lady we would like to have identify them in a line-up."

"Fine with me," came the reply.

40

"We demand a lawyer here in Panama!" Louisa shouted.

"I'm afraid," began Gonzolez, "as far as we are concerned, you never arrived here in the country."

The security guards dragged Dan and Louisa to their feet.

The cold handcuffs bit into her wrists.

INSIDER TRADING

Most management consultants are not above bragging from time to time about the size of their hefty paychecks, impressive wine collections, or distinguished European sedans. However, few care to mention the hours they put in at the office to reap such monetary rewards. Thus it was that Alex Steele came to be working at his desk in the London offices of Bane Consulting Associates at 3:18AM.

A tall and thin man, Steele slouched forward in his wrinkled gray pinstripe suit as he worked. Five years ago, upon graduation from business school, he had been blessed with 20/20 eyesight. Now, thick reading glasses rested upon the rim of his nose: his corneas a sacrifice to quest for wealth. From time to time his eyes lost their ability to focus on the tiny figures dancing across his computer screen, and he had to look away, close his eyes and rub his temples. The sudden ringing of the phone, surprisingly loud in the silence of the deep night, jerked the consultant away from his computer.

"Steele here," his voice raspy after hours without use.

"My friend. We could use an update." The American voice was surprisingly clear despite originating thousands of miles away.

"The decision has been made. It is as you feared."

"What! So soon, but it is only two months into the project. I thought you consultant guys would drag the thing out for at least six months. You do get paid by the month don't you?"

"Yes", Alex began to explain. "But you see, the conclusions are often made quite early on. Then we go back and fill in the supporting detail until we are confident that we will be retained for the implementation phase of the project."

"That's backasswards…almost criminal!" The man on the other end of the line sounded quite angry now.

"Hey don't blame me. I'm only the Engagement Manager. If you have a problem, take it up with the Partner. Anyway, I thought you guys were paying me for information, not for doing my job."

"You're right. Is there anything else specific you can tell me?"

"I can do even better than that. I can email over to you the working draft of the final presentation that will go to the Chairman and the Board at the formal meeting in March. Of course, releasing such data increases the risk to me. If you want it, I will need my fee doubled." Alex looked out the window, and waited anxiously through a moment of tense silence.

"O.K...double. But I expect continued updates for such a large...retainer. Send it."

Steele smiled, hung up the phone and opened his desk drawer. Pulling out an anonymous 'burner' phone, he hit 'send' and the essence of the document scattered into bursts of static firing through the phone lines to their very important destination. Picking up his briefcase, he walked down the hallway to where the two Associates and three Analysts assigned to his team were working around a large conference table. A score of empty coffee cups, soda cans, and take-out food containers littered the room. One of the Analysts was asleep, her head on the table, blonde hair spilling into the leftovers of her Thai curry dinner.

"All right soldiers," Steele began, putting his glasses back into their case. "Let's wrap it up for the evening, I think we have all done enough work for one day." After all, he thought to himself, I just made $50,000 in pocket money for sending an email.

Penelope Shawl, President of UCBS Securities, stood up, walked over to the door to her office and slammed it savagely. Turning hard, she walked back to her desk and sat down angrily in the great black leather chair behind it. Closing her eyes, she slowly counted to ten until the rage subsided somewhat. The arrogance of these people, how could they be so stupid!

Spinning her chair around, she faced the great city of New York which stretched out northwards from her perch on the 103rd floor of the Freedom Tower. All the power she had amassed over such a long period of time, and it was to be stripped away! The first woman to rise to the very pinnacle of a major investment bank, and to think it would all be lost because of some damned consultant.

Shawl looked down again at the sheaf of papers held in her hands. The quality of the phone photos of the document was poor. However, the title itself was quite clear in its import:

United Canton Bank of Switzerland:

The Need for Investment Bank Division Divestment

Presentation to the Board of Directors

Project Saffire

Bane Consulting Associates

August 15, 2022

There were still great gaps in the presentation, but the conclusion was relatively complete and detailed: Faced with massive loan losses in its home market of Switzerland as well as significant reparations to Holocaust survivors, UCBS was faced with the choice of selling either its asset management or investment banking divisions so as to rebuild its capital base. While both divisions were profitable and growing, neither was large enough to survive on its own and it was more than likely that staff cuts would be severe at the division unfortunate enough to end up on the auction block.

Bane concluded that as U.S. stocks had recently experienced a major bull market, it was better to jettison the Investment Bank Division at what was likely a market top rather than be forced to downsize operations when the inevitable bear market arrived. In contrast, the Asset Management Division was seen as a long-term growth business that fitted well with UCBS' core competency of private banking services.

It all made perfect sense. Except of course that many of the conclusions were based on flimsy assumptions, and much of the data backing up those assumptions had yet to even be fabricated by Bane, much as less inserted into the draft document.

UCBS Securities had been built almost from scratch by Shawl and a small cadre of loyal minions over the last decade. Managerial autonomy and a cut of a massive revenue stream equaled power for Shawl, and she liked the power. The sale of the division was would be painful. Independent, the new firm would have difficulty bringing in deals without the AAA backing of the parent Swiss bank. Sold off to a larger firm, and Shawl would likely find herself looking for a job. Wall Street was not known for hiring women, no matter how competent, for top management positions. 'No', she thought to herself. 'I'll do whatever it takes to keep what I've got.'

Shawl picked up her phone and hit a speed-dial button. "Allen," she began calmly. "I got that damned email, and I've calmed down. So when you are ready to tell me whatever else you have, come on over."

In less than one minute, Allen Roberts, UCBS Securities Head of Equity Products, entered the office. He was a decade older than Shawl's 40 years, but as a self-made, self-educated man from the Bronx, he had already gone far to reach his current lofty position. He pulled off the jacket of his trademark poorly cut and wrinkled suit and slouched into the expansive leather couch which was centered under a large original Monet landscape.

"No fucking surprise, eh?" he began. "Those consultants are a bunch of bastards aren't they. I bet they actually enjoy throwing underpaid grunts like us out of work."

Despite herself, Shawl smiled. Roberts had terrible manners, was even less polite and could be a real boor. However, he was a pro at making money and so while he certainly was a SOB, he was UCBS Securities' SOB. "So how about your back-up plan?" she asked.

"I think we have a real problem there, and you ain't gonna believe why. Christian is outside - O.K. if he comes in?"

Shawl frowned and paged her secretary. The door opened and Christian Mansuch strode into the room. The Head of Firm Security's suit was a perfect charcoal, his bearing almost regal, the dark red silk tie subdued as always, his steel gray hair perfectly tamed. 'Great looking guy' Shawl thought for not the first time. "Good morning Christian," she said. "Care to have a seat?"

"No thank you Ma'am. I prefer to stand."

"Well at least that hasn't changed. So what have you found for us today?"

Christian opened the hand-tooled deerskin portfolio he carried and began to read from his notes. "Our friend, Mr. Jonathan Eden, the partner from Bane in charge of the Project Saffire study has had a very quiet past, except for one thing."

"Last time I checked, it only takes one good skeleton in the closet to come up with an effective blackmail," Shawl added.

Christian sighed. "I prefer the term persuasion Ma'am. However, I am not sure this...skeleton is of much use to us. You see, it appears that Mr. Eden had a friend during his MBA years at Wharton in the early 1980s. A very special....male friend in fact.

46

"You mean he's gay?" asked Shawl. Roberts nodded.

Christian continued, "Oh yes, he is quite out of the closet. Not a big deal in and of itself."

"So what's the big deal?"

"His special friend at Wharton seems to have been a Mr. Gregory Net. I believe you are acquainted with the gentleman?"

"What?" Shawl blurted out. "That's unbelievable!" Shawl had never liked the President of UCBS Asset Management, but he was a male chauvinist pig, made homophobic jokes and was married with three children. This was truly shocking.

"Well it is quite hard to prove of course Ma'am. We have several classmates who were willing to speak to me about the matter, but only confidentially. Certainly these two men were, and are still, at least friends and so it is unlikely that Mr. Eden would want to recommend that our Asset Management Division be sold if it would lead to Mr. Net's unemployment."

Shawl leaned back in her chair and pounced. "Fine, why not blackmail...persuade Mr. Eden to change his mind in terms of the recommendation or we will blow Greg's cover. I'm sure Mrs. Eden would be interested in learning of her husband's past."

"Yeah, well that's a problem," answered Roberts. "You see before she became Mrs. Net, she used to be a Ms. Greenfield and she was in the same class at Wharton. So she probably knows as much about Greg's extracurricular activities as we do. I thought about spreading the information to the Board, but while they may be uptight and Swiss, I can't believe they'd fire their beloved Asset Management chief just because he might be a bit light on his feet."

"I see your point." Shawl pursed her lips for a moment. "And if we go to the Board and tell them that Eden is a friend of Net's and thus not impartial we might be seen as acting petty. But there must be some way to get to this guy. We can't just roll over and get slaughtered!" The Investment Banker composed herself for a moment and then looked straight into the eyes of her security chief while speaking slowly and firmly so that she would be understood with complete clarity. "I want you to do whatever it takes to produce the desired change in Mr. Eden's conclusion."

Christian nodded. "I have been thinking Ma'am. What if Mr. Eden weren't Mr. Eden?"

Shawl raised an eyebrow.

It was a warm May afternoon and the exit doors to the Mendocino Community Playhouse had been thrown wide open. An breeze flowed through the auditorium and carried with it the smell of the sea. Rehearsals for the upcoming Summer run of Death of a Salesman were in full swing, and the Director had just called a five minute break. Jack Sanford, cast in the lead role of Willie Lowman, stepped outside for a quick smoke and a moment of quiet contemplation. Leaning against an old redwood he gazed out across the Pacific and idly watched as the clouds crawled southwards through the sky.

"Mr. Sanford. May I have a moment with you?"

The actor turned with a start, he had not heard anyone come up behind him. But there stood a tall, well-groomed man in a dark business suit with steel gray hair.

"Ah...sure. What might I do for you."

"I have been retained to ask you to play a certain important role in an upcoming event."

"Well, I am flattered. But my contract here runs through the end of the Summer," said Sanford as he pointed up at the black-lettered marquee.

"Yes. Might we discuss my proposal over in the car for a moment?"

Sanford looked over the stranger's shoulder and saw a black Mercedes limousine in the grassy parking area in front of the playhouse. 'How big a role was this?' he thought to himself.

Sliding into the back seat next to the stranger, Sanford nodded to the driver who was cut off from direct contact by a glass partition. The stranger opened up a leather portfolio and handed the actor a photograph.

"We are quite interested in having you play the role of this man - in real life."

Sanford looked down at the photo, and then back up at the man next to him. Searching his face for some sign of emotion. There was none. "Well I certainly look a great deal like him. Except maybe for the nose."

"Oh, we would take care of that Mr. Sanford. Allow me to explain with a bit more detail. We want you to impersonate this man during a meeting in August of this year. You will dedicate every waking moment in the interim learning to act, walk, and speak like this man."

"I'm sorry, whatever your name is-"

"Call me Frank," interjected the stranger.

"O.K., Frank. You see I have a contract for the lead role in this play right here in Mendocino and will not be available until the end of the summer. And besides, this job sounds a bit fishy."

"Let me discuss our terms. We will pay you $125,000 now. We will pay you $125,000 at the conclusion of your performance." Sanford's jaw dropped, but Frank did not miss a beat. "We will pay all room, board and travel expenses. We will pay all medical expenses-"

"Medical expenses for what?"

"Cosmetic surgery. And upon completion of this contract we will pay to have your appearance changed back to its original form if you so wish. You will also never speak of this role to any living person, now or in the future."

"But what about my commitment here?"

"Mr. Sanford, it is my understanding that you are to receive $125 per performance of Death of a Salesman. You have $350 in your Wells Fargo savings account, and an additional $37 in your checking account. We are offering you a quarter of a million dollars for less than four months of work. Finally we are offering you the greatest test of any actor: you must actually convince an entire audience that you are another person. I doubt you can afford to turn us down." Frank's stare was intense, and the actor wavered only for a moment.

"Can I have a half hour to get my things together?"

"Someone will be sent back to collect your belongings. We leave now."

The limousine pulled out onto the road and sped away.

Jonathan Eden ran through the morning drizzle and eased himself into the back seat of the Range Rover sent by Virgin Atlantic Airlines to ferry him off to his flight at Heathrow. He had already started working when the driver pulled out into traffic, winding through the serpentine, pedestrian-choked asphalt that passed for roads in The City of London. Eden was looking over the presentation he had to make to the UCBS Board in Zurich that afternoon. While it was too late to make any real changes to the large packet of reports in his briefcase, it never hurt to go over everything one more time.

A moment later, another Range Rover pulled up at the same curb and the driver held up a sign reading 'Mr. Eden'. It was to be a long wait.

The Bane partner looked up from time to time as the views changed from the gritty urban, to the melancholy suburban that passed for scenery in this part of England. Just in the middle of double checking a cost-of-capital calculation the consultant was surprised as the Rover stopped suddenly and daylight ceased flooding in through the windows. The back door was wrenched open, and a man stood there holding a gun to Eden's face.

"Good morning Mr. Eden. Would you mind stepping out of the car?"

Eden looked into the eyes of the short man behind the gun and spun to look at the driver.

"You best do what he asks," said the man behind the wheel in an American accent. The consultant stepped out of the car, and looked around at the empty warehouse into which he had been driven. The driver also exited the car, and continued, "I am afraid we will need your clothes and your luggage Mr. Eden. And please strip quickly. We would not want you to miss your flight."

Eden's emotions swung quickly back and forth between fear and anger. He looked up at his treacherous driver and noticed that the man's gray suit and wingtip shoes were a bit too expensive for someone who ferried people to and from the airport. "My flight?" he asked dumbfounded.

"Yes, your flight," replied the driver as he pointed towards a darkened figure who even now was walking forward to emerge from the shadows.

The great castle rose up from the top of the mountainside towering above all who dared to stand below. Six hundred years old and never stormed, its essence of stability and strength was well suited as the symbol of UCBS. The bank's wealthy Private Bank customers needed no more than to glance up from the shores of Lake Geneva to be assured that their money, their legacy, was safe.

Penelope Shawl leaned against the parapet a thousand meters up, drinking in the grandeur of the view. Behind her a five meter long window looked in on the main Boardroom where, even now, the other members of UCBS' elite were gathering. Out of the corner of her eye she saw Eden/Sanford enter the room, mingling with the bank executives, pumping hands and smiling confidently. 'This is it,' she thought to herself with a tight intake of breath. All the hours of the actor's practice based upon surveillance tapes and videos as well as the best plastic surgery that money could buy were now to be put to the test. Seeing that the subterfuge appeared to be working smoothly, Shawl relaxed and walked into the Boardroom.

A few moments later, the two dozen members of the Board began to take their seats around the massive mahogany table. Most were tired old men who owed their sinecures to the generosity of the Aixes family that owned more than 10% of the bank's stock. 'Yes Men' they were, one and all. Every chair was filled now except the conspicuously empty one reserved for Mr. Gregory Net. Shawl smiled to herself: the carefully planted slow leak in the front right tire of Net's limousine must have done the trick. Undoubtedly he would make it to the meeting - after all how long can it take to change a tire? But, this one final detail ensured that Net would not have time to mingle with Eden/Sanford before the meeting. Shawl worried whether or not the act would hold up under such intense inspection.

Julius Aixes, Chairman of the Bank, brought the meeting to order and minor points of protocol were discussed. It was then that Gregory Net, President of the Asset Management Division, the great computer whiz, the King of the Quants, arrived and took his seat. He was out of breath, and there was a streak of black grease along his hand and the cuff of his

52

white shirt that poked out from under his suit. Shawl had to restrain another smile thinking of her colleague helping the driver to change a flat tire.

The first major item on the agenda was taken up by Gunter Fueron, President of the Swiss commercial bank. His proposal, to make one massive provision to the loan loss reserve so as to 'clear the desks', needed a two-thirds approval of all voting members present. Fueron argued that to continue the current gradualist policy forced management to constantly focus on fighting yesterday's fires rather than focus on the offensive in an attempt to gain domestic market share. The vote passed easily 20-0 with four abstentions (Shawl and Net both in the latter category). The domestic bank was sacred of course due to that division representing the original core business of the Aixes family in the 1700s.

Next came the discussion as to how this massive provision was to be funded. The Chairman puffed himself up and began, "As you know, we have been contemplating the need to raise capital for some time. It was decided last August that one of our two U.S. Divisions would be sold. This is why we have retained Bane Consulting Associates to conduct a thorough industry and strategic study to help make the difficult recommendation as to whether we should dispose of our Investment Banking or Asset Management Division. Mr. Eden, have you completed such a study and are you prepared to make your recommendations at this time?" All eyes turned to the consultant.

"Indeed we have," began Eden Sanford in an eloquent upper-crust British accent. He passed out copies of a thick report to each of the Board members. "From the very get-go the answer to Project Saffire seemed quite clear to us: that Investment Banking is a cyclical business moving into a general secular decline." He glanced over at Shawl who did her best to look as if she was only concealing her anger with difficulty. Net beamed and held his head as high as one hailing from southern Connecticut could. "However," the consultant continued, "as we delved ever deeper into the project, it became evident that we had been mistaken. In fact, the risk-adjusted returns from the Investment business are expected to be lower in the long term due to the synergies generated between the corporate customers of the Commercial Bank being cross-sold Investment Banking products. In fact, it is quite expected that investment management companies are now trading at what may be once in a generation valuations and we would recommend a relatively speedy disposition to insure that UCBS receives the highest possible price for the unit."

Most of the Board members were studiously looking through the graphs and tables contained in the report. This also allowed them to avoid meeting the eyes of Net, whose face was darkening with anger at this turn of events. Shawl eased back in her chair, and allowed herself to savor the moment.

"This is absurd," Net began. "We…all of us here who have spent so much of our time in this industry. Why are we allowing our decision to be directed by a consultant, a dilettante who knows nothing of the sweat and tears we have poured into this company? Both the Investment Banking and Asset Management Divisions are gaining share in a growing market segments. Why don't we consider downsizing the Swiss Commercial Bank? After all, it is losing money in what is in effect a zero-growth economy. Why throw good money after bad? Let us look to the future, not the past."

"But don't you remember that you recommended Mr. Eden to me personally when we were hunting in The Black Forest this winter?" Aixes was clearly angry now, the thought of gutting the domestic bank was anathema to him.

Shawl narrowed her eyes. This connection between the Net and Eden had always seemed just a bit too coincidental to her. It had been a set-up all along, and Aixes had gone along for the ride. Clearly, the Chairman could care less about

54

which of the two U.S.-based divisions should go, but when push came to shove, it might as well be the one run by Shawl. The old Swiss man had never been happy with a woman so high among them.

"And I also remind you that we are the ones making the decisions here Mr. Net," Aixes continued. "I for one am ready to cast my ballot. Are there any more comments?" The room was silent and tense. "Then we shall vote on the subject at this time."

"If there is any further need of me, I will wait out on the balcony," Eden declared.

"All in favor of sale of the Asset Management Division", the Corporate Secretary proposed. 22 hands were raised. Only Net and Shawl remained motionless, glaring across the table at each other. She looked up and watched as, out on the balcony Eden lit a cigarette and inhaled deeply. "All those against?" Net raised one hand weakly into the air, accepting the futility of his action. "The required two-thirds vote has been sustained and entered into the record."

Aixes swiveled and addressed the only woman in the room. "Ms. Shawl. I trust that you will be able to find a buyer for the Division in a reasonable amount of time?"

The Investment Banker turned to the Chairman. "Yes sir," she began, "in fact I would expect that we will be able to complete a sale within 60 days. In preparation of this eventuality, I have made discreet enquiries and believe I already have three potential bidders lined up who are eager to perform due diligence."

Aixes straightened up, visibly impressed. Net stood up and left the room.

The Corporate Secretary moved onto the next order of business, but Shawl hardly heard as she watched with growing apprehension as Net appeared on the balcony and confronted Eden/Sanford. If the actor's true identity was discovered now… Net was yelling, and his face had grown red against the blondness of his hair. However, no sound penetrated the double-paned glass. Suddenly, Net lunged forward forcing Eden backwards violently against the Parapet wall as he gripped him with both hands around the throat.

The Board members rose from their seat at the altercation, but before any of them could make it to the door, the ancient masonry of the parapet gave way and the two men tumbled out of sight.

Shawl was one of the last to reach the balcony wall. The two figures lay in a crumpled heap far below. She let out a short involuntary laugh as the thought 'Talk about killing two birds with one stone' flashed through her mind. Luckily, she was not heard over the commotion of the agitated businessmen around her.

The next morning a hotel limousine drove Shawl directly onto the airport tarmac to where a corporate jet was waiting. Christian Mansuch stood silently next to the boarding ladder.

"Morning Christian."

"Good morning Ma'am. I heard about the unfortunate incident at the castle. It does somewhat complicate the situation of our house-guest in London."

"Yes, quite. And how is he?"

"Oh safely under lock and key Ma'am."

Shawl climbed up the ladder to the entrance of the plane before turning to address the man who waited on the tarmac below. "And Christian. Would you see to it personally that the body is never found?"

The security chief stiffened noticeably for a moment before replying, "Yes, Ma'am."

"Good," she said turning, mounting the stairs and disappearing into the plane.

FRAGRANT HARBOR

Colonel Ricardo Silva, Acting Director of Brazilian Naval Intelligence squinted through the window of his car at the smog and filth of Sao Paulo. The air quality was even worse than usual due to smoke from yesterday's riots in the favela slums. It was hot but while the masses shriveled in the heat, it was wonderfully cool inside the long Mercedes. Besides personal safety, many of the wealthy and important in Brazil demanded bullet-proof cars because thick glass and oversized engines promised the best movable climate control possible.

As the Mercedes proceeded at a steady rate through downtown with an ensign at the wheel, Silva attempted to relax in the back seat. One of the good things about the coup and the declaration of martial law was the creation of street lanes for exclusive use by military vehicles. Good thing too, thought Silva, it would not do to be late for today's meeting. The generals running the Junta chose to reside in safe and orderly Brasilia. However, most of the operational forces had to spend their time in the teaming and sweltering industrial urban centers where the threat of armed opposition from poverty-induced unrest was always close the boiling point. Thus, when General Constans, the number three man in the junta, came to Sao Paulo and summoned all intelligence chiefs to a meeting it was no time to dally.

The car passed through a security checkpoint and then pulled up in front of the entrance to the grand palace where two military police in starched fatigues and glistening steel helmets stood stiffly. Both snapped to attention as Silva emerged. After a final identification check, the Colonel was escorted to a high aerie of a conference room where the city, in all its hazy glory, stretched out on the far side of the large picture windows. Most of Silva's counterparts from other departments had already arrived. A moment after he sat down, the last two attendees, Chano, of the Ministry of the Treasury, and Constans himself arrived. Chano took the seat next to Silva, as their superior stood at the head of the table.

58

"Gentleman," Constans began, "the situation is not good. Since the collapse of our currency in 2019 this great nation of ours has been in a deteriorating spiral. Two years since we took over, and we are failing to restore order to the country. As you know, inflation is once again rampant, our currency continues to weaken, and foreign investment has slowed to a trickle. The result is growing lawlessness among the urban poor, a rising narcotics trade, and the resumption of activities by leftist guerrillas who were thought to have been eradicated decades ago."

"Our economists tell us," Constans continued with a slight nod towards the Treasury Minister, "that our best chance is a wave of massive privatizations which will rationalize the economy and increase economic growth. In addition, the funds raised from selling these assets will fill our coffers so that we can increase the level of bread and circuses provided to the lawful and bullets to those who are not. Our investment bankers are ready to float our remaining stakes in TeleBras, PetroBras and ElectroBras as well as most of our ports and, railroads as well as Banco do Brasil. I expect that I do not have to stress the importance of returning our nation to peace and economic growth or we will never be able to return control to the idiot politicians."

"So what can we do? None of us are economists," asked Ruban, the head of the powerful internal security forces.

"Our largest problem is east Asia in general, and China in particular," Chano began as Constans settled into a chair. "These nations are preparing to raise more than a hundred billion dollars from the global equity markets in the next twelve months alone. Various portions of Indonesia's telecommunications, the State Bank of Vietnam, the Bangkok Subway System, the Port of Shanghai and the People Liberation Army's stake in China's largest national cellular phone service are all up for sale."

"There is only so much equity capital floating around out there and we will not be able to get good prices for our national industries if these deals are allowed to come to market! They have order, or at least more than we have here in Latin America. They also have larger populations which represent greater latent demand. Their savings level is higher to marry with international investment to increase economic growth. But this is only a matter of degree. We offer fantastic opportunities to new investors at this point: monopoly status, tax holidays, inexpensive labor, free security and locations close to vast stores of raw materials. But even so, we lose out because we do not rise to the level of Asia. Therefore, I believe we must lower Asia to a level below that of ours".

"How can we do this?" asked Ruban impatiently.

"By reducing the attractiveness of the East Asian Pacific Rim, and by making those markets appear to be riskier than ours," answered Silva.

"Exactly," agreed Chano. "And while I do not know specifically how to accomplish this, I expect that you, our colleagues from the intelligence services, would have some ideas." Silence settled overt the room for a moment.

"Sir, if I may," began Silva. Constans nodded his head in the naval officer's direction. "As a man of the Navy, I was trained to think about scenarios where one was attacking an enemy fleet, and how one could best damage an opponent most severely with the most precise but least expensive weapon. I believe I may have an idea that may match just what you wish to have achieved.

Silva described his plan in less than five minutes. Chano's eyes grew wide, and Constans immediately approved the project with one only caveat - no members of the armed forces could be involved, and there must be no way the operation could ever be linked to Brazil. The meeting was adjourned.

Hernan Canterra sighed in contentment as he looked out at the sparkling turquoise of the Caribbean on a sun blasted day. The beach here on Cuba's Isla of the Pines was all his, except of course for Cindi who was kneading his shoulders, and Marisol who lay on a beach blanket at his feet. Both women wore matching blue bikinis which seemed to make the contrast between Cindi's ginger fairness and Marisol's African darkness all the more stark. The sun beat down on his head and the massage was making him drowsy Life was good except for the thirst that crept up on him all at once.

Luckily, however, Luis had just walked down from the house with a chilled bottle of Mexican Bohemia beer - Hernan's favorite. The first swig was wonderfully bitter and cold and refreshing.

Luis waited till Canterra had savored his beer for a moment and then announced, "A Senior Silva has arrived to see you sir."

"Thank you Luis, please escort him over to us. And insist he have a beer."

"Certainly, Jefe."

Silva, tall and dark, and wearing rumpled slacks emerged from the house moments later holding a bottle of Bohemia.

"Ladies," Canterra began, "would you mind taking a short stroll. I have to attend to a little business."

Marisol and Cindi strolled away as Silva arrived. Canterra smiled as he noticed the shimmer of envy wash over his guest as he looked out at the departing women.

"Señor Silva, this is quite an unexpected pleasure. It has been years since we last met." This of course was because the Brazilians had not needed a discreet assassin since resumption of martial law. Unwanted political opponents were simply be arrested or 'disappeared'.

"Yes, yes that is true," replied the Brazilian. "But I am aware of your successful endeavor in the Yucatan and back in Sao Paulo we were all quite impressed." He was referring, of course, to the bullet that Canterra had put in the brain of the Mexican President a couple of years back.

"Thank you sir. Now what brings you here today? Pleasure, I hope. I would be happy to lend you a pair of swimming trunks, and of course there are many lovely ladies on this unspoiled little island."

"I am afraid not. I have come here today on a matter of somewhat urgent business. I need to commission you for a project, one that will regrettably result in a large number of fatalities. I will leave the execution of the assignment up to you as long as the requisite results are achieved. In return, we will be happy to pay you your normal fee, plus all reasonable expenses."

"I am listening," Canterra replied.

The sun beat down on the waves.

The first presentation began at 8:00AM, but Hong Kong's Lucky Dragon Shangri-La Hotel was swarming with portfolio managers. And why not? It was that time of year when the investment bank unit of Debit Lyonnais held its Annual Asian Investment Update - a three day seminar ostensibly geared to allowing executives of major East Asian corporations a chance to pitch their stocks to some of the most influential asset managers in the world. Of course, the event had grown to be much more - a place where everyone arrived for something other than just the chance to watch aging men drone on at a podium. The salesmen and bankers of Debit Lyonnais got a chance to push deals and commissions with their best clients, portfolio managers got a chance to mingle with each other and line up their next job, and corporate managers were wined, dined and offered an assortment of women and drugs and young boys in their palatial suites, courtesy of the event's generous sponsor.

This, the newest 'Shang' in Hong Kong, was well situated for such a conference, straddling the waterfront of the great city. From its windows one could look north across the world's largest toilet bowl of the Fragrant Harbor to Kowloon City, and the great expanse of China beyond stretching over almost unfathomable distances of desert, plain and mountain. And in the fetid water itself, crouching at the hotel's foundation scurried the ever-moving collage of shipping representing all the steaming island ports of the rest of Asia - craft hailing from Mindanao, Java, Formosa, Oahu, Ceylon, Ache and Singapore.

Little had changed since the communist takeover of the former British territory. The red flag now flew from prominent buildings and peaks, statues of Queen Victoria had disappeared quietly, and an additional level of corruption had descended upon the business dealings of the city like heavy motor oil poured over a smoothly running engine block. Debit Lyonnais paid more than in pre-1997 to hold the conference. New taxes, excise fees and outright bribes placed in sealed red envelopes were exchanged discretely. In return, the conference had grown and become the largest of its kind in Asia and offered unparalleled access to management personnel in PRC-owned corporations. And even with the phenomenal growth in the rest of east Asia, China was still the hot growth hope of western capital: three billion of everything - underarms needing deodorant, ears needing cellular phones, feet needing basketball shoes. That most significant companies were partially owned by the Communist Party, or the Peoples Liberation Army, mattered little as it insured minimum competition and maximum corporate pricing power. Of course one always had to look past summary executions, forced abortions and the occasional seizure of poorly connected western assets, but what are such trifles when there is money to be made.

Deborah Chasen awoke as the pilot of the Singapore Air 747 announced the imminent landing at Hong Kong's new Chek Lap Kok International Airport. While born and bred in Boston, she had traveled to this part of the world so often that she hardly cared to take in the view of the city below through the tiny window. A year shy of thirty she was the only female passenger on the plane who would have been able to pull off wearing one of the tight-hipped sarongs of the smiling Singaporean stewardesses. "I hate this airline!" she cursed to herself as a petite beauty helped a Japanese businessman put his shoes back on. "I'd like to see them put their male stewards in hot pants, and hire some bozos who made it to the last cut for a cologne advertisement."

She closed the top of her notebook computer, and looked at the business card taped to its cover:

Deborah Chasen, C.F.A.

Deacon Asset Management

Senior Portfolio Manager

Asian Equities

1175 Avenue of the Americas

New York, NY

It had been a long and sometimes lonely road, but just looking down at that card sometimes made up for all the long plane flights, late nights, and missed dates. After all, she now oversaw close to three billion dollars for one of the largest and most prestigious institutional asset management companies in the U.S. Many claimed that one had to live in Hong Kong, or maybe Singapore to effectively manage Asian assets, but Deborah knew better. Maintaining an expensive global network of offices filled with Expats on Cost of Living Adjustments made little sense, especially when New York was the true center of global financial information.

However, one did have to visit on-site from time to time. First Class trans-Pacific airfares to HK were expensive, but each round trip ticket cost less than a month's rent for a nice apartment in this crowded and obscenely congested corner of the world. Deborah slid the computer under her seat just as the landing strip bounced off the wheels of the 747. As the plane slowed, the windows looked out on what looked more like a military installation than one of the world's largest commercial airports. Passenger traffic to Chek Lap Kok was still far less than the facility's capacity, and so the PRC stationed much of the region's combat aircraft there. This was supposedly to utilize the space better, but many knew the real reason: a show of force for all who flew into Hong Kong that the Brits would not be coming back, that the South China Sea was the PRC's lake, and that Taiwan had better not think too hard about independence.

Deborah was escorted swiftly through customs by a Debit Lyonnais representative who had bribed the correct personnel, and she was shown outside to a waiting limousine. A young Caucasian man sat behind the wheel, a gold hoop earring in his left lobe.

"Where to, Miss?" he asked, in standard cockney.

"Lucky Dragon Shangri-La, please."

"Of course Ma'am," he replied already pulling out into traffic.

Amazing how quickly a Brit's role had changed in this place.

Canterra strode along the docks of the Port of Manila. It was not long before he found the ship he was looking for: The Pride of Cebu was an ugly little gasoline tanker painted dark gray which floated high in the water in the absence of any petroleum in its 20,000 gallon capacity hold. While ugly, the ship was in fine shape. Canterra was generally pleased with the almost military bearing of its captain, a Mr. Negros, who was more than accommodating due to the high rate paid to charter The Pride.

In less than a half a day, the ship's crew of six had filled 15,000 gallons of high octane aviation fuel into the tanks and was steaming towards Hong Kong. Why Canterra wished to deliver a cargo to a port where the product was readily available was a mystery to Negros, but he cared little to investigate, as long as he was paid well.

The Pride wallowed a bit in the lee of the rising swells as the prow aimed towards the setting sun. The skies were clear and the ship handled better with a full belly, pushing the prow lower into the dark water. As Canterra sipped a cold Coke on the forward deck, the wind in his hair, he smiled, hoping this would be his last contract. While if successful, his talents would be even more in demand than before, the fee was high enough that he could keep himself quite comfortable for many years to come.

Winston Chambers of Chimera & Spineford Investment Management settled into a seat in the back of the conference room. It was 9:00AM on the third and final day of the DL Conference and the young analyst was more than slightly hung over. As usual on Thursday nights, he and some of the lads had been out for a few pints in Wanchai. Only nine months had passed since his graduation from Oxbridge and the opportunity to hang out with some of the brethren helped to assuage his gnawing homesickness for the green isle of his birth. Of course, one did not turn down the opportunity to work for C&S, among the oldest and most prestigious of Britain's fund managers.

The current speaker up at the podium was a Mr. Baimbung, President of Samproerna, an Indonesian company primary engaged in selling highly addictive clove cigarettes to young Javanese. Luckily for Sampoerna, Indonesians did not usually live long enough to develop lung cancer, and so the litigation problems endemic to UK and US tobacco companies, were mostly absent here. Winston followed consumer goods & services companies in SE Asia, and he currently rated Samproerna a 'Buy' inside C&S. His main concern for the stock right now was whether or not Philip Morris' new joint venture (partly owned by the Indonesian President's youngest son) was going to be able to gain significant market share. Unfortunately, Samproerna had been quite tight lipped on important data points such as the subject of price cuts, frequent smoker trinket award programs and the purchase of convenience store chains.

The formal presentation was, as usual, taken up with the CEO reciting the history of the company which was already well-known by most of those sitting in the audience. Winston slouched in his chair as he waited for the Q&A session to start. As he looked up he saw that babe manager from Deacon named...Deborah, sit down a few seats away. Winston had tried to get her to go out with him the night before but she had turned him down. Despite Ms. Chasen being a bit older than the young C&S analyst, Winston thought he had a chance. He possessed a striking similarity to the young Roger Moore, and was known by most of the lads as 'The Saint'. The accent, the looks, the prestige employer: he thought he could convince Ms. Important to a little roll in the hay. Winston had already learned that these conferences were excellent hunting grounds for lonely young lovelies who were far, far away from home. He had already bet HK$100 with his colleague, Ajax Farthington, in favor of his success. No time like the present, once more into the breach, and all that.

"Care for a smoke, Ms. Chasen?" Winston offered quietly as he sat down. She quickly shook her head, 'no', as she looked down at the pack of Indonesian clove cigarettes. However, Winston noticed just a hint of a smile pass across her face.

"You don't really smoke those things do you?" she asked.

"No, of course not, but it looks good to light one up with Baimbung in our private meeting later today."

"You get to meet with him separately?"

"Sure, most of the companies here take the time to come up to our suite on the top floor." Deborah's face was a mixture of envy and anger. Winston was mostly telling the truth. C&S did have private company meetings in a private suite - but the room was paid for by Debit Lyonnais which also set up the meetings. The only reason C&S received such treatment was a result of his employer directing a huge amount of commission dollars DL's way after each conference.

"You coming to the gala dinner tonight?"

"Yes...Winston," she replied reading off his name tag (though she actually did remember his name quite well). But I don't know how late I will stay, I hear that after the surprise speaker the thing usually degenerates into a big cloud of cigar smoke emanating from a couple of hundred drunken men."

"Ah...sounds like heaven to me." Once again, he thought he caught the slightest bit of a smile on her face. Better make sure she ended up assigned to his table. One of his friends at DL would make sure of that.

Security men from several different nations and private firms began scouring the Shangri-La as the sun reached down towards the waves. Every year security at the conference became tighter, but few minded. The portfolio managers got to feel important, corporate and political speakers felt relaxed enough to have a few drinks and open up, and Debit Lyonnais gained the reputation for throwing one of the city's most exclusive parties.

Don Gordon, Managing Director of DL Asia, stood up against the great plate glass windows of the third story rap-around bar. At six four, two hundred and fifty pounds, with red hair and ruddy skin, he certainly stood out as a Yank. His firm did not really like having a non-Frenchman running its most profitable unit, but no one back in the Paris headquarters wished to interfere with a phenomenal success.

While all had gone well up to, the last day of the conference, Gordon was a bit concerned. Every year the conference had an increasingly impressive surprise speaker. This year would be no exception to the trend. Unfortunately the entourage for the all-important show stopper was expected to arrive at 5:30pm, and already it was close to 6:00. While there were clients lounging around the bar to be mingled with, Gordon could not turn away from the window just yet.

His eyes were drawn to the sky which was turning a spectacular shade of orange from the mixture of the setting sun and the monstrous amount of pollution in the air. All across the teeming city, taxis were idling in traffic, water ferries were straining against great loads of commuters and small cooking fires were heating greasy evening meals. The sun burned red, and huge crows soared on the thermals of the remaining day as they waited for darkness and the chance to rummage undisturbed through Hong Kong's refuse. The great

Bank of China Tower, its red pennant radiantly backlit, shifted its shadow and cast the Shang into semi-darkness.

Finally, Gordon saw three large limousines pull up to the rear entrance of the hotel. The man for whom he waited alighted from the middle car and, surrounded by security, disappeared into the hotel. The American turned around and strode over to the crowd gathered over at the bar; there was schmoozing to be done.

Winston Chambers stood politely when Deborah Chasen appeared at his table. Luckily, she was a bit late and the seat to Winston's left was the only one still vacant. She returned his smile for just a moment and then introductions were made with the rest of the table's patrons. All were male and in their forties: a few other foreign asset managers as well as the CEO and the CFO of a large Filipino manufacturing conglomerate.

The massive dining hall was filled. More than 600 diners were decked out in black tie and evening gowns as overly attentive waiters buzzed among the groupings draining cases of fine French wine into waiting glasses. The harbor through the windows was alit with a kaleidoscope of lights from moving ships and the towers of the Kowloon shore. Security guards, also in tuxedos, with radio earpieces spiraling down into their jackets, stood stiffly at the door with hand-held metal detectors. Even the two bomb-sniffing German Shepherds wore small black bow ties around their necks. The food was excellent and abundant with caviar, sirloin, lobster tails, pheasant and wok-fried baby vegetables. Small goblets of sherbet to cleanse the palate were provided between each course.

In spite of herself, Deborah found that she was becoming a bit tipsy and having a good time. The air of festivity was finally given a point of focus when Don Gordon rose to stand at a large and imposing podium on the stage at the southern end of the hall.

"Good evening ladies and gentlemen. Thank you for attending and aiding in the success of the eighteenth Debit Lyonnais Annual Asian Investment Update. Here tonight, we are more than 300 portfolio managers from around the world controlling in excess of three trillion dollars. In addition, we have more than 100 Asian corporate managers here who oversee firms with assets in excess of seven trillion dollars. And, finally, there are a few score of us here from Debit Lyonnais tonight who are of little consequence whatsoever." There was a warm, wine-induced chuckle from the crowd at this.

"I hope not to bore you, so I will keep things brief. We have a very special guest tonight whose views will undoubtedly be quite influential to the development of the region. After that, we have a couple of bands lined up to get you dancing, and the bar will stay open until...well, until the last of you leaves."

"So with that, I would like to introduce tonight's speaker. A man who needs very little introduction: Mr. Xi Jinping, Chairman of the Chinese Communist Party, and President of the People's Republic of China!"

There was a hush across the room. Astonishment showed on many usually jaded or cynical faces. At first, most thought the announcement must be a joke. But then, as several bodyguards escorted someone who at least looked a whole lot like the Chinese leader down the aisle towards the podium, applause roared up from the chamber. A few held back, thinking that the man before them must be a professional impostor, or a comedian. But, as the figure at the podium looked across the room, all doubts melted away: this was a man of power and strength, who easily held the fate of more

71

than a billion Chinese in his palm and whose military forces cast long shadows across the Pacific and Greater Asia.

"Good evening," his voice was deep and his English surprisingly good to a crowd who had previously only heard the man speaking in Mandarin. "I come here tonight to invite you to join in what will be the event of the 21st century; The maturation of the Chinese economy to the point where it will stand on the same plane with those controlled from Washington, Berlin and Tokyo! Many politicians may watch with trepidation as my embattled nation struggles to throw off centuries of oppression and take its true place on the world stage. However, I know that you in this room are here to make money, not war or diplomacy or treaties. And to you - Fat Choi! Let us get rich together!"

Deborah looked over at Winston's face as the applause began to roll like thunder around them. Her eyes twinkled mischievously as she leaned over and, almost kissing his ear, whispered: "How badly do you want me?"

Winston sat up in shock. His eyes locked onto hers, and for a moment, the young man's shield of coolness fell away from him.

"You can have me if you want, Winston. But only if we go right now. You have ten seconds to make up your mind."

The Brit looked back at the powerful man speaking at the podium. He was clearly torn. In the end, animal instincts won out over an Oxbridge-trained quest for knowledge. "Ok Deborah. Let's go," he whispered back. "But let me get one thing straight. Who's picking up who here?"

"Oh, you are picking me up Mr. Chambers. Just remember, my being on top is part of the deal."

The Pride of Cebu chugged into sight of Hong Kong Island just before complete darkness settled over the sea. As the tanker closed in on the port, a Customs motor launch came alongside. With a quick review of charter papers and lading declaration along with an even quicker exchange of a few hundred U.S. dollars and the Filipino ship was allowed to pass. Another few miles of sailing and The Pride came into view of the lights of Central. It was time for Canterra to go to work.

He unlocked a briefcase in his quarters and removed two small boxes each about the size of beer can, a roll of gaffers tape, and what appeared to be a normal cellular phone. He also removed from his kit a silencer which screwed neatly onto the automatic pistol holstered under his jacket.

On deck, it was dark enough for him to slip, unnoticed, over to the main cargo bay. In seconds he unscrewed the round hatch that opened into the dark, sloshing mass of aviation fuel below. He then dropped one of the cylinders into the fluid and taped the second to the inside of the hatch before cranking it closed. Now came the hard part.

The engine room of any large ship is a hot and noisy place, and the Pride of Cebu's was no exception. The two men working there never even heard Canterras' approach nor the bullets that killed them. The chief mechanic died in his bunk happily dreaming of the beaches of home. The first mate died in the Head in an embarrassing state of undress. Captain Negros and the final crewman were the last to go. As they died, they left the floor of the wheelhouse slick with blood.

Canterra's timing was almost too good as the ship was passing the Shangri-La. He took control of the wheel, and slowed the engine, turning the wheel until the Pride of Cebu was aimed directly at the great hotel which cast its bright lights harshly down onto the black water. As he pulled the tape out of his pocket, he heard the sound of a pistol being cocked behind his head.

"Hands in the air, Mr. Canterra," came the voice from the rear of the wheelhouse. A few steps, a reaching hand, and then someone had two guns and somebody else had none. Canterra turned around slowly to find himself facing a short but muscular Asian dressed in a black wetsuit still glistening from the water of the harbor.

"What are you doing on this ship? And how do you know my name?" asked the assassin.

"My name is Chao, I am here to watch you Mr. Canterra. As to how I know your name...well in Taipei we take an interest when someone known to us as a paid killer arrives in the neighborhood and charters a tanker. Or should I say, a sailing bomb?"

"Taiwanese security?"

"That's Republic of China to you...sir. But, essentially, yes."

"So what's the plan Chao?"

"Oh, I am just here to tag along. After all you have a job to complete."

"I work alone!"

"I insist," Chao moved his gun ever so slightly so that its target moved from Canterra's chest to his groin.

"Fine." The assassin turned back to his work. With the wheel taped into place, and the throttle set to Full Ahead, the ship lurched forward and thrust itself towards the buildings of the waterfront.

"I don't know about you, but I'm leaving."

"After you Mr. Canterra."

The two ran down to the deck and lowered the tanker's Zodiac motorboat into the water.

"So Chao, you going to kill me here?"

"Oh no. That way no one would ever find your body, and then we might be blamed for the murder of the Communist Chinese Premier."

Canterra looked quickly at the hotel which they were rushing towards. "You mean to say he's in there."

"In there? He's the guest of honor. I guess you should have asked for a larger fee. Get in the boat!"

Several guards stood along the waterfront promenade of the Shangri-La. Most were alert and scanning, but none noticed anything abnormal about the Pride of Cebu until it was within a few hundred yards of the hotel. After all, ships had been coming and going all night, and this one did not seem out of the ordinary.

The armed guards ran towards the railing, yelling at the ship in a Babel of languages. Seconds later, after no response, they opened fire. Unfortunately for the guards, their bullets were unable to penetrate the double-hulled tanker to strike at the volatile aviation fuel within.

Inside the grand ballroom, the Premier had finished his speech and was taking questions. A short and scrappy American hedge fund manager from San Francisco had asked, "We have heard about localized military mutinies occurring in the north and west of your country as well as food riots in the coastal cities. Are these reports true, what are you going to do about it, and why should we invest in your country when you can't even keep the people fed?"

"Rude bastard!" Gordon thought to himself. "Have to make sure he isn't invited next year."

Xi Jinping drew himself up and turned visibly darker. His amplified voice became so loud that one could hardly hear the sound of gunfire. "We will maintain order in China! We

will move forward, and no one shall stand in our way!"
Security guards were holding their hands to radio earpieces
and running through the crowd towards their specific
charges.

In the Zodiac, Canterra slowly pulled the cellular phone out
of his jacket. Chao watched closely, his pistol never
wavering. When the assassin pushed the power button, the
phone chimed and lit up in his hand. "So, I guess I can't be
caught or I might tell the police that you Taiwanese knew
about my activities but did nothing to stop me.

"Oh, I disagree Mr. Canterra. You can be caught, but I
doubt you will be in any condition to talk when you are
found."

Canterra pushed three buttons on the phone. The sound of
the tanker's prow plowing into the concrete of the promenade
reached out across the harbor. "That's what I thought," he
replied and pushed the 'Send' button.

The 15,000 gallons of aviation fuel detonated in an
awesome orange-red blast that ripped the entire front off the
first ten stories of the hotel. The concrete of the promenade
was blown apart throwing huge chunks skyward, and a
fireball followed the flying shards of glass into the ballroom.
Bodyguards threw themselves onto the Chinese Premier so
that he was one of those lucky enough to survive the initial
explosion. He looked up to see pieces of furniture, slabs of
pavement, smoldering fires and body parts all around him.
Blood was flowing from his ears and he felt dizzy. He felt
more than heard the screams around him. Only one of his
bodyguards was still alive, and his right leg was broken. The

Premier staggered to his feet, but was then thrown down again as the entire building shifted on its shattered foundation. Through the gutted windows the fetid water of the harbor poured in. He, and a few others raced towards the rear doors, but a bore of oncoming water ripped them off their feet and slammed them into the floor and walls.

Chao was almost thrown off the Zodiac by the blast. His vision was wiped out by the flash, and he immediately slipped into a crouch expecting Canterra to attack. However, as Chao's vision returned, he realized that the assassin was nowhere to be seen; all that remained of his prisoner was the cellular phone lying on the floor of the boat. The Taiwanese waited quietly for his prey to come up for air. He heard nothing. Wait! There was a ripple in the water off to the right. Chao raised his gun and took aim. As he did so the cellular phone exploded. The Zodiac's engine and occupant were blown into the air, and the boat filled with water and sank silently into the night.

A few moments earlier, Deborah rolled off Winston in the queen bed in her upper story hotel room. He got up and walked, naked, over to his pants lying on the chair by the window. Fishing a clove cigarette out of the pack in the front pocket, he lit up and was staring out the window when the bomb went off. Flying glass ripped through his body and into the walls and ceiling. The shockwave threw him across her naked body on the bed. Deborah was miraculously unharmed as she was shielded from most of the force of the blast by the interior wall, low position of the bed,...and Winston. Stunned for a moment, she looked down at his pleading eyes. Blood flowed freely from his neck and a dozen other places. He tried to speak, but a rasping noise was all that came out. The building shifted on its foundation and shards of glass slipped off the furniture onto the floor. Deborah picked up the hotel phone, but there was no dial tone. She slammed it down into its cradle. Winston pointed to his cellular phone on the night table. She smiled at him, picked it up, held it towards his face to unlock it, and dialed.

"Yes, Morgan Stanley? This is Deborah Chasen. I want to make a trade for my personal account - number 47-676984. Yeah, I want to short the Hong Kong Market. Use Hang Seng Futures. Margin me out all the way. Every penny...Right. Great. Thanks. I'll call back later for the confirms."

Winston's eyes glazed over and blood trickled out of the side of his mouth.

Canterra boarded the Singapore Airlines flight to San Francisco, his head completely shaved, and his pinstriped suit neatly pressed. A very good fake US passport was in one jacket pocket, a First Class Boarding Pass in the other. Exhausted, he fell back into his seat: It had been a long swim to Kowloon.

"May I offer you a glass of Champagne, Sir?" asked a smiling stewardess.

"By all means."

The next morning, pictures of the gutted Shangri-La hotel were prominent on the front page of most major newspapers around the world. The leadership of China retreated into vicious backroom fighting to decide on a successor for the slain Premier. Asian stock markets plunged in value and the

Dollar gained against the Yen. Pundits on US financial news programs decried the riskiness of investing one's hard-earned money in the overly risky south-east Asian region.

Goldman Sachs and ING Barings announced plans to bring several Brazilian privatization issues to market in the next few weeks. An intense roadshow was planned for London, New York, and Tokyo among other cities.

Riots broke out in the streets of Changsha and Beijing. Western news agencies offered conflicting reports as to the reasons for the disturbances. 'Democracy' seemed to be the chief demand of the protesters in the street. The top general of the PLA appealed for calm on national television, but the next day there were reports of fighting between opposing military units in Manchuria.

The 8th Army of The Republic of China landed and seized Shanghai in the face of little resistance. President Lee, speaking from Taipei, announced that the Nationalists was returning to the mainland to bring 'Democracy' to all of The One China, and that the communists had lost the Mandate of Heaven. A short bitter battle was fought on the outskirts of Tianjin between loyalist PLA forces and a coalition of mutinous mainlanders and the Taiwanese.

It was all over in less than a week. Like so many other repressive regimes throughout history which had rotted to the core, the PRC collapsed into dust. The capital of the Republic of China was officially relocated to Beijing where President Lee announced that free local elections would be held in 12 months time and that massive privatizations of state-owned industries would take place as soon as possible. The Shanghai and Hong Kong stock markets soared in value, as did Taipei's and Seoul's. The dollar lost much of the value that it had recently gained, and the 'smart money' was again rumored to be heading east.

Goldman Sachs and ING Barings announced a 'temporary withdrawal' of the Brazilian offerings 'until more favorable market conditions prevailed'.

Deacon Asset Management's Asian Equity Product reported the top investment performance in its peer group due, primarily, to a well timed short of several east Asian markets and currencies, followed by a reversal resulting in large long positions.

Winston Chambers was buried in a quiet, green cemetery near his parent's home in England.

TIME EQUALS MONEY

Ron Nelley rolled over in bed and slammed his fist down on the clock radio to turn off the alarm. Overly bright sunlight streamed in through the slats in the window blinds, dappling the bedroom with a zebra pattern. Helga stirred in her sleep, and Ron kissed her lightly on the cheek before pulling himself out of bed and walking out onto the porch where he lit up the first cigarette of the morning.

Inhaling deeply, the lanky young man relaxed as he looked at the sweeping view of the Pacific Ocean from the second floor of his Mission Beach townhouse. Surfers were already shredding waves in the early morning high tide, and a mosaic of dog walkers, joggers, and rollerbladers maneuvered for space along the boardwalk. A few stared at Ron's naked form as they passed, but most gave no more than a passing glance: after all, this was San Diego.

The Marlboro done, Ron moved back into the house, and within twenty minutes, was dressed and ready for work. The Audi roared to life, and glided out onto the road. The cellular phone system came on by voice command, and Ron plowed through almost all of his 34 messages by the time he rolled into the La Jolla parking lot housing his employer: Hamilton Investment Management, the New York-based mutual fund company. The San Diego office was staffed by Ron, his analyst, his trader, and a secretary/office manager.

Dark wood paneling and a sense of quiet greeted a visitor to the first floor office where Ron sat behind a large marble-topped desk. Rather than the standard flashy, high-rise office space used by most investment firms to impress clients, Hamilton's so-called 'Health Science Investment Center' existed solely to keep Mr. Nelley happy. One of the most talented (or some said, lucky) health care stock pickers ever to play the game, Ron had forced Hamilton to set him up in his adopted home of San Diego where biotechnology companies seemed to breed and grow like mushrooms in a dark, dank basement. While unassuming in its appearance, the small office was where more than three billion dollars in the Hamilton Health Sciences Mutual Fund was managed at an annual expense fee of 2.25% representing a juicy profit centers in the great Hamilton Empire.

This serious responsibility appeared to weigh lightly on Ron as he settled in for the day and scanned through the lists of stock tickers glowing on his computer screen while slurping noisily at a hot latte which had been waiting on his desk when he arrived. A few moments later, Alicia, his secretary and recent former captain of the UCSD woman's windsurfing team, appeared with the Wall Street Journal and a large, stiff Bloody Mary.

"You got more Worcestershire, right?" Ron asked.

"Take one sip, and you tell me," she replied.

"Mmmenhhh," Ron let out in great satisfaction seconds later. "That's how I like 'em."

Alicia smiled and looked down at the schedule in her hands. "You have the management of Pfizer coming in at 10am, Pat from Alex, Brown coming by at noon to take you to lunch, and Amino Design Labs at 3pm."

"Great," he replied, looking through his file cabinet-size humidor for just the right cigar. "If the rest of the day holds up like this, I won't be complaining. The computer screen told the story: another day and the biotechs continued to surge ahead for the second year running while the big drug companies continued to see their prices under pressure since their recent speculative peak. This matched Ron's fund positioning just fine as other health care portfolio managers fought among themselves for second place in the mutual fund rankings.

Life could not have been better for Nelley, until just before the Pfizer meeting when his hands started shaking uncontrollably and he lost vision in one eye for several minutes. In fright he stood up, and pitched over as if he were drunk.

The doctor at the university hospital was calm and collected while drawing Ron's blood and moving through a complete neurological exam, but behind the brave front both patient and physician were tense. It was clearly unusual for a young and healthy 32-year old to exhibit such symptoms.

Ron was subdued that night when he arrived back at the apartment. The sky turned a riot of purples and pinks as the sun went down over the waves. Pensive, he sat in the balcony deck chair fumbling with his car keys when Helga came up behind him and draped her arms around his neck. He drew the beautiful Chinese woman down into his lap and kissed her long and hard. When they came up for air, she smiled at him happily and his concern softened and drifted away.

"You looked unhappy sitting there all alone," she said to him. Her bright red silk scarf flapped in the breeze, setting off the dark charcoal gray of her business suit. "Is there anything wrong?"

"No," Ron replied. "But maybe it is time you gave me a full checkup."

Helga giggled as he carried her into the apartment.

The doctor's office called back three days later with a message that the lab results were ready. Ron was afraid he already knew the diagnosis: he had had more shaking fits, and his speech was sometimes slurred. However, the expectation did little to soften the news.

"Ron, I'm afraid you aren't going to like these lab results." Nelley leaned back on the paper-covered examining table which let out an embarrassing loud crackling noise in the hushed room. Dr. Green was a strong man who was able to look Ron in the eye as he went on. "It seems that you have inherited Huntington's Chorea from one of your parents despite the fact that neither ever showed symptoms themselves. As you know Huntington's is passed on by a parent holding one defective gene - there is a 50% chance of each child contracting the disease. It is non-curable, and is characterized by increasing loss of motor function and often the onset of dementia. The bad news is that this condition is progressive, the good news is that most patients loose a good deal of weight over time, and so you can throw out those diet books." The doctor looked down at the lanky portfolio manager and continued, "However I guess that is little help in your case."

"Well, I'm going to go out and eat Cajun every night for the rest of the week," Ron replied with a small forced smile.

"Yes, well for treatment at this time I would recommend Chloromazine 50 mg and Haloperol 4 mg both three times a day to help control the loss of motor control."

"How long do I have?"

The doctor paused a moment before making a reply. "In most cases, this disease takes several years to run its course. However, due to the severity of the onset of your first visible symptoms I am concerned that your case could potentially progress much more rapidly. I would suggest that you make sure that your affairs are in order. Now may I ask, have you experienced any unusual changes in your mental state? Have you noticed any shift towards paranoia?"

"Doc., I play the stock market for a living: I'm always paranoid."

"Well yes. Look, keep me up to date. You can pick up your prescription at the hospital pharmacy, and I want you back here in two weeks. And Mr. Nelley…I'm sorry."

"Yeah," the patient replied, looking at his feet, forcing down a burning in his throat. "Me too."

Ron fired the Audi down the flat strip of pavement. The wind whipped through his hair as the speedometer pushed through 90. He passed a Highway Patrol car, but the cop watched impassively from behind dark shades. "The guy must know," Ron thought to himself. A few moments later, the Portfolio Manager pulled into his office lot. In a pile under his desk he found the prospectus for Plasmid, Inc., a small biotechnology company attempting to raise $120 million in a secondary share offering.

"Alicia!" he yelled out to his assistant who looked up from her desk at the summons. "Call that company Plasmid for me. Tell them I want to meet with the CEO in their offices first thing tomorrow morning. Ron looked out at the great redwood tree which proudly dominated the center of the office complex's courtyard. Its serenity, strength and age seemed almost a direct mockery of man's ephemeral life.

The flight to San Jose was uneventful in that each year the short-haul service resembled less a relaxing plane journey more and a crowded city bus. Luckily, Ron held Platinum status on United, so he was allowed an assigned seat and the right to board the plane early before the bleating mob filed past him straining under the weight of their ever larger carry-on bags.

The drive to Palo Alto took Nelley through the energetic urban sprawl along Route 101 in Silicon Valley. The headquarters of Plasmid, Inc. was located in a low-rise R&D building 'on the wrong side of the tracks' where the railway line evenly divided the town between Stanford-centric luxury and the somewhat seedy area along the great north-south highway. The drab exterior of the building disguised the hi-tech slickness that lay within. Corporate offices were laid out on one side of a long hallway that stretched the length of the building. On the other side, a ceiling to floor glass partition allowed one to look in on the 'clean' rooms on the other side where masked workers in white gowns performed various tasks with expensive-looking machinery.

Nelley was escorted into an office almost as tidy as the workspace behind him. Greg Yuan, the company's CEO, stood up from behind a desk to shake his hand. Yuan was a tall man fresh out of Stanford's Biotechnology department. In fact, his company had been almost entirely financed by the University and local 'angel' money. However, the cash burn at a modern biotech firm was such that in many cases the options were either a success in the capital markets or total failure - and that is where people like Ron Nelley came in to the picture. The two men sat and exchanged pleasantries for a moment before getting down to business.

"I have two main questions for you today," Nelley began. "I want to know more about the technology you are trying to harness, as well as why you guys are having such a difficult time raising the cash you need?"

Yuan was full of energy and he leaned forward across his desk and began to answer almost before the question was finished. "OK. So while I imagine you know a bit about what we are trying to do here, let me just review the basic concept for a moment: Our process, if successful, should be applicable to many inherited conditions, but we are starting with Huntington's due to the orphan status of the disease as well as the already known location of the defective gene

86

which causes the illness. We start out by building the entire patient's genome set on a supercomputer, pump through some massively-parallel processing to rebuild the DNA without the defective gene, create a string of genetic material called a plasmid, introduce that into a bacterium, breed the thing in bulk, and Shazam!, you have something that can be directly introduced into the patient's system that will reverse the degenerative process of the disease."

"But not a cure?"

"No, but we imagine that only five to ten treatments would be necessary over an increasingly extended period of time, until a complete remission was achieved as the incubated plasmid material overwhelms the defective material with which the patient was born." Yuan leaned back and smiled.

"Sounds prohibitively expensive for one cure at a time?"

"Yes, for the first couple of patients of course. But we expect that there will be a steep decreasing cost learning curve, that the process can be significantly automated over time, and that the entire process can then be transferred to curing those with other genetic conditions. Our expectation is that an entire patient treatment regimen could fall to $25,000 and we can easily charge $100,000 for the treatment. With 1 out of every 100,000 contracting the disease, we are talking about more than $175 million in tax-free profits just in the U.S., and that's just for Huntington's"

"But I guess that 'the street' doesn't believe you?" Nelley asked holding his arm down against his side to hide a tremor that passed through his hand.

"Yes," Yuan replied with a sigh. "But if we can't afford to go through with adequate Phase II and III trials, we will never get FDA approval, and then all this technology, so close to application will remain dormant. We already reduced the deal size from $200 to $120 million to cut some corners and move forward more slowly, but a couple of sell-side analysts have come out with skeptical research reports on the process, and our stock has fallen from $8 to $6 as a result and scared off some potential investors."

There was silence in the room for a moment, as Nelley looked down at his hands. He did not look up when he finally spoke. "I'll buy the whole deal, $200 million worth - a third of the company at $5 per share, on one condition."

"Yes?"

Nelley looked up, his gaze intense. "That you run full throttle starting today to work out the bugs and complete the process. And that I be in the first cohort of test subjects."

Yuan looked into Nelley's eyes. The shock in the young executive was clear. But he only hesitated a moment before putting out his hand across the desk to the portfolio manager. "Deal."

This time the shake was extra firm.

It was only three days later when Dick Robertson got wind of the Plasmid deal. Nelley's first mistake of the morning was to actually pick up the phone when it rang. The ex-SEC lawyer, now resident pain-in-the-ass at Hamilton Investments, was on the other end of the line.

"Ron, its Dick Robertson. We have a bit of a compliance problem here. It appears that you just bought this stock, Plasmid, which is now 10% of your fund, and that we own more than 10% of the company's net worth. Both are violations of the prospectus. I hope this is a data entry error?"

"No, Dick, your info is correct. But this is a great company, and I really think we needed to put some capital on the line here. The risk reward ratio is fantastic."

"Maybe so Ron, but the rules are black and white. We can get sued for something like this. I'm afraid you are going to have to dump some of those shares."

Ron felt the anger bubbling up inside of him. He took a couple of deep breaths. "Look. Why don't we talk about this in person? I can be in the office tomorrow morning around eleven. Why don't we talk then?"

"Fine, but I don't see how that will change things."

After another moment Nelley hung up the phone and yelled out to Alicia. She appeared in the doorway a moment later.

"Alicia, get me on the red-eye flight to New York. I'll need the suite at the Waldorf for early morning check-in so that I can take a shower before going into the office.

Hamilton Investment's New York office took up several floors of prime midtown office space. Robertson's personal office perfectly matched his sense of self-importance. A large picture window faced north to overlook Central Park, and his wall was decorated with photos of the obese lawyer shaking hands with assorted luminaries, Lucite plaques announcing mergers and acquisitions long since failed, and framed newspaper clippings showing insider traders of the 1980s being led away in handcuffs.

Nelley sat in the chair set up in front of the desk and grimaced. What this guy had to do with running a successful investment management company was lost on him. The lawyer's main job was to say 'no' to any request. Each day Hamilton was not sued, was a day of success for Hamilton. If Robertson had been around at the firm nine years ago, the Health Sciences Fund probably would never have been launched.

Robertson finally came back to the office and shook hands with the portfolio manager before taking his seat and jumping right in to the matter at hand. "Look Nelley, we both know the rules. You can't own more than 5% of a company, and no stock can be more than 5% of the fund. That's all there is to it."

"Look. I know this is going to be a big stock for me, and I just need to give it a little time. We both know the thing is illiquid. It's trading at $5.75 today, and if I had to dump my position it would probably get pushed down a couple of bucks. That could lead to some real problems for the company, and distract management from doing their job. They could end up spending their time talking up the stock rather than working on new products."

Robertson held up his hands to signal that the argument did not change the situation. Nelley hesitated a moment, and then reached into his inner suit coat pocket to pull out a thick envelope which he placed down on the desk. Robertson looked at the $20,000 in $100 bills inside. Surprisingly, he did not seem the least bit shocked.

"How about we just forget about this little problem for a couple of months?" Nelley asked.

"O.K.," Robertson began, slipping the envelope into his pocket. "But if that stock goes down a buck, your fund will be down a couple of percent and people will start to notice, and then I will have to suddenly notice that there is a problem. Do we understand each other?"

Yes. We do." With that Nelley got up and walked out of the office, trying to put the slime-ball out of his mind. He continued through the corporate maze until he came to Antony Lehman's office. Lehman ran Hamilton's financial services funds and had started at the company, with Nelley, as an analyst. Both had moved up the ranks, though the 'sexiness' of biotech vs. boring old banks meant that the financial fund had never been able to raise even half as much as the Health Sciences Fund.

"Hey buddy!" Nelley yelled out to his old friend who was barely visible behind a pile of financial statements. Lehman looked up and smiled. There were bags under his eyes and his hair was disheveled and thinning. In addition, he had gained a good deal of weight in the last year - he looked a mess.

"Hey Ron. What brings you out here? Need to pick up another bonus check?"

"Oh, just some business meetings. But Tony, what's going on with you, you look like you need a vacation?

The New Yorker sighed, "My performance is down, my girlfriend demanded an increase in her monthly shopping allowance, and I've been working way too hard. Life is too short to go on like this."

"Yeah. You're right," Ron answered with a touch of wistfulness. "But listen, I've got a great stock for you."

"You following banks now buddy?"

No, no. It's a biotech firm like all the others. It's called Plasmid, 'PSMD', over the counter. They are working on a cure for inherited diseases, and I think you just got to buy it. You can buy up to 20% of your fund in non-financials, right?"

"Yeah, and I sure could use something to jack up my performance."

"Put three or four percent of your fund in the thing, say $25, $30 million worth, but don't push the price. It's illiquid so buy it slow over the next couple of months. They won't have another announcement before then anyway."

"O.K. I guess you've never set me wrong before."

"Why don't you put the trade in now. I can wait." Lehman looked up at his old friend for a moment, surprised by the intensity he found in the face across from his. A few years back he would have stood his ground and done his own research before buying something. But New York had eaten away at his soul. He slouched his shoulders and relented. Nelley sat quietly as Lehman typed an order to the trading desk.

Helga surprised Nelley at the airport gate as he arrived back in San Diego. She threw her arms around his neck and hugged him hard. After a moment's shock, he returned the pressure. The embrace felt wonderful, he had not realized the amount of stress he had been feeling. They kissed long and hard, their bodies pressed tightly together. Other disembarking passengers flowed around the couple like rushing water past a rock in the middle of a stream.

Finally their lips parted. "Ron, can we sit down for a moment?"

They arranged themselves on some uncomfortable waiting area seats, but looking into each others' eyes the curved plastic furniture seemed matching thrones.

"I have something to tell you Ron."

He looked at her expectantly.

"I'm pregnant!"

The look on Ron's face was not exactly what Helga had hoped to see. He grabbed his briefcase in one hand, and Helga's elbow in the other. Despite her protests, he refused to speak a word until they made it into her car. Then, with the windows closed, and the gleam and grime of other autos surrounding them, he leaned over and whispered into her ear for a few moments. Both were crying when he finished.

There is nothing like a long vacation in Tahiti to relax the mind and make one forget life's problems. A thatched hut, the great sweep of an inner lagoon with cotton ball clouds racing across a sky that seems impossibly wide. Lolling on the beach, Ron found that he could almost forgot his fate. But the troubling thoughts always came back to him. His marriage to Helga was a concern. Why did she want him now? Now that he was a walking corpse who had not yet remembered to stop breathing? But she certainly was willing and seemed happy to dedicate herself to her lover in his time of dusk. After all, he thought to himself, he would be able to give her everything now and not have to worry about inheritance taxes. For a month they held out, living each day for its own sake, acting as if catching every color of the sunset were the only important thing. However, Ron's condition deteriorated quickly over just a few days: not only did the palsy intensify, but his memory faded in and out, speech become laborious and swallowing increasingly difficult. Plasmid called to say that they had synthesized the genetic material necessary for the first batch of trial patients, and so the honeymooners wearily boarded the plane back to California.

Within a week Ron checked into the hospital. Doctor Green spent a great deal of time with his patient, but again there was little he could do. At the end of the week, he made his rounds through the hospital, and for his last stop, headed towards the room of his youngest patient. He walked with some trepidation: the job was never easy when there was bad news to deliver. The sterile linoleum shone a dull white in the florescent lighting as he finally came to Nelley's room. He looked down the hall and saw his patient's wife, leaning backward to compensate for the child she carried within. The doctor shook his head and entered the room. Inside, the stricken man lay on the bed, his head propped up by pillows. Ron's strong frame had been weakening fast, and his ribs, visible under the gown, were now pushing out from his emaciated body. "Hello Ron."

Nelley found that for a change his voice did not fail him. "Afternoon Doctor…" He paused as the name of his doctor eluded him, as did most things these days. He nodded toward the sheaf of lab results held in his doctor's left hand. "How am I doing?"

Doctor Green sighed and sat down on the chair next to the bed. "I'm afraid Ron that this disease has progressed much faster than I ever would have expected. Often it can take patients years from first noticeable symptom to where you are today. But there is very little we know about Huntington's. We know what causes it, but not much more. There is no way to know if your case will continue to progress at its current speed. You certainly could see a quick recovery. But, I'm afraid that if things continue in this way, then you only have a few more days." The patient's left arm and leg quivered uncontrollably, but his face remained unmoving as a tear welled up in the corner of his eye.

The next day Greg Yuan came to visit. Nelley had completely lost his ability to speak, and his eyes had started to jump around in their sockets from time to time. Yuan was visibly shaken. However, he pulled himself together and sat down in the chair next to the bed. Ron jerked his head around to look at his guest.

"Mr. Nelley. It's me, Greg Yuan, from Plasmid, Inc. Do you recognize me?" The patient nodded his head.

"We are growing some clarified strains of your genetic material right now, but we will need another few weeks. Not that long to hold on now."

Nelley scrawled, "Won't make it" on the notepad in his lap. Yuan looked down at his feet. He looked up as he heard the pen moving across the paper again. "My wife is pregnant" Yuan felt his stomach tighten.

"You realize that there is a 50% chance that the child will not have the disease." Nelley nodded his head. "But, I promise you Mr. Nelley. If your child has the Huntington's gene, and we come up with a cure, he will receive the very best treatment we can provide. For free."

"Thank you," Nelley wrote on the pad.

One week later Nelley slipped into a coma and died. A day after the funeral, Dick Robertson, acting swiftly as the diligent Chief Consul of Hamilton Investments, discovered a serious compliance breach in the Health Sciences Fund. A small biotechnology stock, Plasmid, Inc., represented almost 10% of the fund's assets. A small computer error had kept the information from being relayed to the Compliance Department. Robertson, in his memo to the Chief Investment Officer, noted that Nelley may have manipulated the system to cover up the size of the holding. The next day, Hamilton dumped more than half of the Health Science Fund's holdings of Plasmid, Inc. at an average price of $3.75 per share. The fund immediately fell from first to seventh place in the year to date performance figures for health care mutual funds.

Antony Lehman returned from vacation to find that his 3% position in Plasmid had fallen by almost 50% in value, and there was an e-mail from Robertson inquiring as to why a financial services fund was holding an illiquid biotechnology stock, and that the Trustees were interested in why performance had been slipping. Lehman put his head in his hands. It was going to be a long week.

One month later, Plasmid, Inc. issued a press release indicating that the first human trials of a new therapy for Huntington's was showing remarkable results in 18 out of the first 20 patients having a complete remission from all visible symptoms of the condition. The press release indicated that fast-track FDA approval would be requested and that there was a good chance that the process could be used for several other genetically-transmitted diseases. The stock closed the day at $18.5.

Helga Nelley gave birth to a seven-pound daughter whom she named Alexandra. The baby tested negative for Huntington's.

BEAR TRAP

The mood in the trading room of the Central Bank of The People's Republic of Vietnam was tense, very tense. Currency traders yelled into phone receivers and jabbed angrily at the keyboards of their Reuters terminals.. The room seemed quite humble considering its importance to the country: housed in the stolid concrete block of a more Statist communist era, cables snaked across the floor around shoehorned desks so as to maintain the telecommunication and data links need to maintain a modern economy. There were few windows, and only wan light filtered in as the sun rose over Hanoi.

Ngo Huu Tho, President of the Bank, looked on with growing concern. His thin fingers stroked the wispy white beard that fell to a point over his chest. He was tired, it was much too early for him, but the currency markets never closed these days. Trading wrapped around the world in an ever tightening web that pulled together the globe's economies in which Vietnam was once no more than a sideshow. Unfortunately that had all changed recently and the financial markets were now focused on the Dong, Vietnam's currency. The great speculative hedge funds of the West had declared war, and Tho was caught fighting a battle he knew he could not win.

Nguyen Duan, the chief trader, his face pulled tight in worry, walked up to Tho. "The selling pressure has intensified. At least three new funds have begun shorting our currency in the last hour. We are trying to trade small lots to keep from draining the reserves too quickly, but the strategy is risky and the market could get away from us."

Tho stroked his beard. He had worked together with Duan for more than ten years, and this was likely to be the saddest day of that decade. "Nguyen, may I have a moment alone. I think it is time to call the Premier." Nguyen stiffened, and backed off. Tho pulled out the tiny Sony phone from his

97

pocket and dialed a number few knew. As he did so he shook his head sadly. This whole mess was so predictable, and the politicians had been deaf to his concerns:

When Vietnam attempted to join the club of 'Tiger' nations of newly industrialized nations, the country had been opened to investment, trade and eventually, currency convertibility. So as to promote stability, the value of the Dong was to trade in a narrow range versus a basket of major currencies. For the first several years nothing but success followed and economic growth soared. Scores of multinational firms set up shop in Ho Chi Minh City and western investment funds were raised with the sole purpose of investing in 'The newest dragon of Asia'. A steady stream of hard currency flowing into the nation was used for the purchase of plant and equipment to revitalize the economy and spur exports. Rising living standards also led to the purchase of billions of dollars worth of foreign consumer goods by a Vietnamese population with a voracious appetite for more.

The result was what economists called a rapidly rising current account deficit and rate of inflation. As ever more dollars and yen left the country each year, too many people attempted to sell their Dong at the same time that inflation eroded the value of the currency. Now the Dong was clearly overvalued and the Central Bank, guarantor of the tight trading range, had no choice but to provide liquidity to the market by selling dollars out of its reserves to all who had Dong to sell. While unsustainable in the long term, the situation became desperate only when the big hedge funds got involved. By selling massive amounts of a currency short and betting on a decline it its value, they could bleed a small country's central bank dry of reserves, force a devaluation and buy back the currency to cover the short positions at a lower price thus locking in massive profits.

The Premier finally picked up the phone on the eighth ring. "Sir. It is Tho here. I am afraid the selling pressure I mentioned yesterday has intensified. Our foreign currency reserves are now down to only enough to cover three months of imports. I think it is time that we consider allowing a devaluation." A few steps away Duan lowered his head in defeat.

It was well after midnight on the trading floor of Dolnotov Investments, home of The Pulsar Fund, the world's largest and most influential hedge fund with more than 50 billion dollars in assets. Charles Dolnotov, president of the firm, and personally worth several billion dollars, stood at attention despite the hour. He had never needed much sleep, no more than a couple of hours each night, and that had always aided his favorite pastime of trading the never-closing currency markets.

Dolnotov sipped his tea and looked out the windows at the glittering lights of Manhattan. There was nothing for him to do right now but wait. This trade was going to work though. He could feel it.

The mood on the floor was tense, but expectant. Only a few of the desks were occupied, as just a handful of night-traders were required to burn the night away with Dolnotov. The firm's financial commitment to shorting the Vietnamese Dong was now in excess of three billion dollars. Of course it was unlikely that Dolnotov could lose much more than a few percent in a transaction on a currency that was already overvalued, but one never knew. Five years ago Pulsar lost more than a quarter of a billion going long on the yen. None of the traders forgot Dolnotov's furor that day.

Suddenly there was a victorious shout from the traders hunched over their screens. A collective sound that echoed simultaneously across at least a dozen other hedge funds across the city. Dolnotov smiled as he looked up at the large-screen Bloomberg mounted on the wall: the Dong had broken free from its trading range versus the dollar and was plunging lower and lower down the graph. The headline flashed across the Reuters console:

'Central Bank of Vietnam allows Dong to float. Currency to be allowed to find its own trading range.'

Within minutes the Dong had depreciated almost 20%, and Pulsar could lock in a sizeable profit. The traders all wore smiles - they had been selected for their competitiveness after all. Who else besides a die-hard competitor would live like a vampire to stare at a screen all night? What was better than winning? Once again they had stood up to a central bank of a sovereign nation and faced it down. And the victory would be that much sweeter when the year-end bonus checks were passed around.

Dolnotov returned from the kitchen and boomed out, "Well boys. Start closing out that Dong position. I told you, Vietnam's currency will never get much respect until they get around to changing its name." Laughter filled the room as Dolnotov popped the cork off a ten year old bottle of Moet & Chandon. Foam gushed over his fingers as he took a long swig and passed the bottle to the nearest trader who replicated the gesture. "Gentlemen. If you will excuse me, I think I'll get a little sleep." He walked over to his personal suite of rooms behind his office. The windowless, book-lined walls of the bedroom were insulated for silence. Slipping out of his clothes and into the bed, the billionaire speculator thought of the tomorrow's newspaper headlines: 'Another Victory for Dolnotov'. Smiling, he drifted off to sleep.

Alvin Vertbridge, Chairman of the Federal Reserve, relaxed in his massive bathtub, sighing in contentment as the heat massaged his sore back. On his left, a frozen margarita perched in the custom-built drink stand, to his right was a pile of unread statistical reports. Another pile of the Chairman's already perused reading lay in a slightly damp pile at the foot of the tub. A yellow rubber duck, a gift from his new wife, floated past him as he read. He quite liked the duck but had made her promise never to tell anyone about it.

The combined report from the Departments of State, Commerce, Treasury and Defense as to the recent events in Vietnam commanded his attention. The nation's economic faults since embarking on liberalization and industrialization were many: too centralized an economy, poor infrastructure, suffocating red tape. The final straw was an inflexible exchange rate system that did not allow the currency to reflect market realities or stand in the face of determined speculator pressure. Recent strikes, riots and imposition of martial law could all be traced back to attempting the construction of a modern economy on the back of an unstable foundation. Of course, Dolnotov and his ilk had been the ones to kick away the supports.

This was not the first time: the Malaysian Ringgit, Indonesian Rupee, Korean Won, Philippine Peso, Thai Baht, Brazilian Real and Mexican Peso had all imploded over the years of the last decade. However, fallout from devaluation of the Dong had particularly far-reaching consequences: The US had been building Vietnam up as a potential counterweight to the rising power of China, and a large market for industrialized exports. There was even the possibility of a return of the Seventh Fleet to Cam Rah Bay. Now the consensus was that Vietnam had slipped back at least five years in its economic growth path, and potentially even more if the hard-liner communists were unwilling to give up control and end martial law in the next twelve months. If not, it was unlikely that international conglomerates would pump investment funds into the nation, no matter how cheap the labor. In any event, US banks were likely to write off at least two billion in loans made to Vietnamese companies and government institutions and several large US industrial firms would see their return on investment fall to zero. Citicorp's and Caterpillar's stocks alone had fallen several dollars each as news leaked out to the financial press.

'This has to end', Vertbridge thought to himself. As Chairman of the Federal Reserve, his goal was a stable US dollar as well as consistent economic growth backed by a safe and sound banking system. Assistance in the successful implementation of foreign policy was an additional unwritten doctrine.

'But how?' One could not just stop global capital markets just because one did not like the results. After all, by standing in the way of the speculators, the Vietnamese had lost and their nation's development has been pushed back by up to a decade. But what if the speculators could suffer their own setback, enough to lose five or ten years as well? Vertbridge smiled as the kernel of a plan formed in his mind.

The door to the bathroom opened, and Donna, Vertbridge's wife of six months, entered. A white terrycloth robe was cinched tightly around her youthful fifties-old figure. She smiled her most evil smile as she slipped the robe off her shoulders and let it fall to the floor. "How are you feeling honey?"

Vertbridge looked down at himself and smiled back as his body responded to the sight of her nude shapeliness. "Irrationally exuberant," he replied.

The report fell to the floor as she sloshed into the tub on top of him.

Vertbridge's armed driver pulled the Town Car up to the Federal Reserve Building on Constitution Avenue. The Chairman, sauntered happily out of the car and greeted several staffers, some by name, others simply with a nod, as he made his way into the building and up to the large office where 'the most powerful man in the world' resided by day. A young assistant ducked his head in to say that his guests had arrived in Washington, and were due to arrive at the Fed at 10 am that morning.

At the appointed hour, the Chairman strode down to his conference room. He sat quietly in the chair at the great mahogany table and massaged his lower back as he waited. A few moments later Johan Wurst, President of the Bundesbank in Frankfurt and Yoshi Yakatori, Governor of the Bank of Japan in Tokyo appeared in the doorway with several of their staff members. Yakatori was a short, bony man with thick glasses and an even thicker mop of white hair. His appearance was often unfairly compared to that of the late Andy Warhol. Wurst was tall and distinguished looking. However, he slouched and seemed significantly older now than just a year ago when his wife had died.

Pleasantries were exchanged, and then Vertbridge asked if it were possible for the three to meet alone. The German staff members exhibited expressions of disdain and hurt while the Japanese appeared impassive as they all filed out of the room. The three Central Bank heads settled into chairs around the table where hot green tea waited for Yakatori, and iced coffee with extra cream and sugar had been prepared for Wurst.

"Good morning to you gentlemen." the Chairman began. "Thank you for taking the time to visit Washington. I expect your meetings in New York went well, and I hope the meeting at the White House was not too stressful." The two guests smiled at that.

"As you know, I have spoken repeatedly to you on the subject of my concern over currency speculation and manipulation in the capital markets. While I have no interest in taking steps backward towards more regulation or less legitimate monetary policy, it seems that the central banks of the world should have some say in how their respective economies are run. Massive growth in the resources of macro hedge funds and other speculators in the last decade has far outstripped the ability of smaller nations to hold against their attacks. My great concern is that the time is fast approaching when their power will be such that in piecemeal fashion they will be able to overpower us one by one. Such an occurrence would represent an unprecedented shift in wealth from the working people of our nations to that of a few exceedingly wealthy individuals." The guests nodded toward their host.

"What I am about to propose has been in the planning stages up here for a very long time," the American pointed to his temple. "And I think the time has come for us to act. I propose that we consider embarking on a course of action that will accomplish several goals: break the power of the hedge funds for years, restore the paramount influence of our institutions, and assist in the accomplishment of a significant goal of our nations' foreign policy, all at the same time in a relatively risk free manner." The German and the Japanese traded wary glances, and Wurst turned to address Vertbridge.

"This seems like a very aggressive course of action Alvin. Would it be legal? And what foreign policy initiative are all of our countries' has anything to do with monetary policy?"

"Well, there is certainly nothing illegal about coming to the aid of an allies' currency, is there?" The guests nodded slowly. "And all of our governments are actively attempting to assist India's steps towards greater democracy and open markets, are they not? And we are aware that our governments are considering a grant of several billion dollars next year to India in return for very little in return. I say we ask our friends in Mumbai to help us to set a trap. And I think that the hedge funds will fall right into it."

Yakatori said nothing. Wurst leaned forward in his chair. "And what is it that you would have us do?"

104

Alvin leaned back in his chair, realizing that he had have already won his colleagues over. "How would you like to support the Indian Rupee - for just a few days?"

Dolnotov sat at his desk and smiled at his two visitors. First there was the obese bulk of Steven Hammerdsmith, his right-hand man. Next to him was Augustus Stevens, the aristocratic British head of several hedge funds all named after different wild dogs: Wolf Fund I, Jackal, Dingo, Wolf II, etc. The three of them had the markets in the palms of their hands. Just a few 'off the record' words from either of them to the right reporter at The Wall Street Journal or The Financial Times was enough to have traders the world over scurrying to copy the trades of these three men who consciously promoted an image of investment infallibility. Their blunders rarely made it to the press. Their successes, even when bogus, were trumpeted from every newsstand.

"So what's next, Augustus? We got you in on the Dong. So it's your turn to ante up the next place to make a killing" Dolnotov smiled over at Hammerdsmith. His number two was a combative man who never let Stevens forget a favor.

"Well the US Long Bond is clearly undervalued. I think yields are going to 5%."

"Come on now - Don't give us that stale trade stuff! We have all heard that you are underwater on the Long Bond. Don't expect us to bail you out on that one.

"All right. I was planning to start this one myself, but I guess I'll let you in on it." Stevens handed a small folder from his briefcase over to Hammerdsmith. "The Indian Rupee has only been convertible for two years, yet already it is rising towards real overvaluation in terms of purchasing power parity. I think we could take it out with the right…push."

"But what about all their reserves, I was under the impression that they were extremely large?" replied Hammerdsmith smugly.

"Yes, that is what some have heard," Stevens replied with just a bit of condescension in his tone. "But in fact, as you can read in the documents now in your hand, most of the reserves are actually in gold, and the value of the metal has been in free-fall all year. In fact, yesterday's announcement of a massive new find in Bolivia by Freeport-MacMoran should place even more pressure on the commodity. It seems the Reserve Bank of India's 'weapons' may turn out to be a bit out of date."

Hammerdsmith appeared impressed and looked over at his boss. Dolnotov realized that Stevens had visited today with every intention of broaching this plan to attack the Rupee. There was no way that the currency of the world's largest democracy could be attacked without a concerted effort from the financial community - especially Pulsar. However, it was a good idea.

"Well I guess I may have to add India to Vietnam as one of the countries I will not be able to visit for the next couple of years," Dolnotov said with a smile.

Jill Kurtez moved in for the kill quickly after remaining aloof from the prey for several hours. She sidled up to the bar next to Jordan Macasen, Governor of the Bank of Canada. He had come to Whistler, British Colombia for the annual meeting of the Canadian Banking Association. His wife had stayed home in Toronto, so Jill had made sure to find a reason to head West.

"Like to buy me a drink?" she asked the bureaucrat

"Certainly, Miss…"

"Kurtez, but call me Jill," replied the svelte young woman as she sat down on the adjoining stool, crossing her legs. She smiled at the slightly drunken 53 year-old. "What are you doing here?"

"Oh, I'm attending a little conference, and thank god, the dinner finally broke up. I'm Jordan by the way."

She held onto his hand just a little too long after the shake had ended and replied, "Yes I know."

"So what are you drinking?"

"I'm finding that I'm not thirsty anymore." Macasen allowed an involuntary look of distress to cross his face.

"What do you say we go for a little drive?" she asked.

Macasen was speechless for a moment, and then simply nodded as he was led by the hand out the front door. The valet quickly brought around Jill's gun-silver 700-series BMW, and they drove off into the cold white of the mountain's shadow.

"So where are we going," he asked almost sheepishly as the car turned down a small, dark side-road.

Jill pulled the car to a stop and killed the engine. "Oh I thought here would be just fine." Her painted nails smoothed through her blonde hair and came to rest on the upper clasp of her blouse. "I thought that if I got into the back seat that you might be able to help me get some of these clothes off.

The Governor was shocked at first, but soon became extremely helpful.

Workers in the foreign exchange trading room of the great Italianate stone palace of the Federal Reserve Bank of New York were controlled, careful, and deliberate in their motions. Who wouldn't be if Alvin Vertbridge, the most powerful man in finance, or the world even, was looking over your shoulder. Balding, and a bit stooped, his eyes were still bright and missed nothing as they followed the action around the room.. Extremely warm and a bit dank, 'The Cave', as the trading room of the FRBNY was known was in one of the old gold vaults hundreds of feet below the Lower Manhattan location of the building. This, the nerve center of the free-world's financial system, was wired with systems shielded with lead against the danger of an Electro Magnetic Pulse that would emanate from any nuclear weapon detonated in the city above. Four armed guards stood at the door. No trader had been allowed to leave the building since the battle for the Rupee had begun a week ago. Anyone who left the room was escorted to and from the bathroom, the showers, or even the jerry-rigged dormitory.

The level of anxiety rose as the President of the New York Fed appeared, with the veins in his nose standing out from the scotch coursing through his body.

"So how are we doing Alvin?"

"Very well, thank you. We are up to leveraged bets of almost $500 billion shorted against the Indian Rupee! We have no idea how many hedge funds are involved, but the number has grown greatly in the last couple of hours since we got the IMF to announce that they would under no circumstances disburse any funds to support an overvalued currency."

"How much have we disbursed?"

"Oh, about $100 billion." The Chairman smiled, "more than the market capitalization of Ford, and GM combined. It must be driving those Hedge guys nuts!" His laugh reverberated off the rock walls.

A few miles north, in the gleaming tower offices of the Quasar Fund, Dolnotov was pacing. Numbers were not adding up, and that was not the way he played a trade. His personal assistant sashayed over to offer him a cell-phone.

"Stevens?"

The pout on his assistant's collagen-spiked lips never changed as she nodded and handed the phone over.

"What do you want, Augustus?"

"You know what," the annoyed voice crackled through the line. "The damned Indians should have been out of reserves yesterday, and they just came in against us on an additional $5 billion! This just does not add up…unless of course, you are trading against me."

"You are a piece of shit Gus!" Dolnotov yelled into the phone prompting Hammerdsmith and every trader to look up and smile. It was always fun to watch the boss get mad, as long as you were not the object of his ire. "Do you know that? I am completely tapped out on this piece of shit currency, the shorting of which was your stupid idea in the first place! If we don't win this one, I am going to march over to your shop and wring your neck until your eyes come right out of your head. I don't care if I am remembered for killing you rather than supporting democracy in eastern Europe, so go to hell!" With that he threw the phone into the corner where it shattered.

Dolnotov motioned Hammerdsmith to follow him into his office. They both sat down and said nothing for a moment.

"What do you think Steven?"

"Screw'em. There is no way they can hold out much longer, and with their reserves exhausted when they fold, there will be nothing left to support the banking system. The currency will just go down that much more. Remember, sometimes you just have to be a pig."

Dolnotov looked out the window, ran his hand through his thinning gray hair, and said nothing.

Jill Kurtez walked out of the Toronto's King Edward Hotel and slid behind the seat of her BMW. Shooting off down the street, she lit up a cigarette and inhaled deeply. Jordan had almost been good tonight, she thought to herself as the speed-dial on the cell-phone chimed away. Within a moment she had Dolnotov on the line.

"Hey Charles, I think I might have something for you."

"Well it would be about time. I have paid you a damned mint for nothing so far!"

"Hey don't get mad at me big boy. How am I to help it if the guy doesn't have any secrets to disclose.

"O.K. Look, I am under the gun here - so make it fast."

"Fine," Jill was becoming seriously annoyed. "I asked him when he was going to take me away somewhere sunny, and he said 'maybe in just a few days as soon as the Yanks are done with Operation Bear Trap'. I asked him what he meant by that, and he shut up right away and he made me promise not to tell anyone. - That's why I called you. What do you think Charles?

There was silence on the other end of the phone line.

"Charles?"

Faintly in the background Jill could hear a man yelling…

"Stop Everything Now!" boomed Dolnotov as he raced into the trading pit from the back of his suite. "I want us out of every short on the Rupee. Go long if you can, I could care less about the spread, just do it!" The traders, assistants and Hammerdsmith looked at their boss incredulously for a moment. But only until, at the very top of his lungs, Dolnotov screamed, "NOW!"

One of the Fed traders in The Cave hung up his phone and turned to Alvin Vertbridge: "Sir, my contact over at Citicorp tells me that someone, probably Pulsar, has started reversing huge short positions on the Rupee." The trading room fell silent.

Vertbridge thought for a moment, then decided to act. "Listen up everyone," he pleaded as if he did not already have everyone's complete and undivided attention. "I think we have played this hand long enough. Go into the markets and start buying every Rupee that you can." Turning to his two Special Assistants, he continued, "You know what to do. Issue the press release, and call the Bundesbank and the BOJ so they can get in on the fun.

Stevens got on the line as soon as he heard it was Hammerdsmith calling.

"What is going on over there. I hear you guys are wimping out?"

"Look Augustus. I do not have time to explain, but you have to reverse your trades! Dolnotov has someone on the inside who thinks this is a trap. We are getting out now, and I would advise that you follow."

"A trap? Who would set a trap? I think you guys are just getting yellow at the wrong time."

"Oh crap Augustus...It's too late now. Look, I gotta go."

Stevens dropped the now lifeless phone to his side and turned as an astonished chorus went up from the members of his trading desk. He bent over to read what everyone was finding so interesting on the Bloomberg:

Joint Press Release From The Federal Reserve Bank of the United States, The Bank of Canada, the Bank of England, the Bundesbank, the Bank of Japan, and the Reserve Bank of India:

In the interest of maintaining global financial stability. It has been determined that the Indian Rupee has become significantly undervalued. As such, the issuers of this statement will begin supporting the value of this currency by engaging in purchases in the open market from all interested sellers.

Stevens suddenly found that he was having difficulty breathing.

As the sun came up over Manhattan, Vertbridge leaned back in his seat. The reports in front of him indicated that the central banks had netted profits of almost $8 billion from the short squeeze, and that several large banks had cut off lending to a score of hedge funds that were now likely to be declared insolvent as a result of ruinous losses. Pulsar was rumored to have been able to turn their trades around, and so glean a small profit, but that one hedge fund was clearly an exception. The Chairman looked over at the exhausted figure of the President of the New York Fed and smiled broadly as he asked, "What do you think? Good enough for government work?"

The curtain fluttered in the breeze from the open window in Augustus Steven's office. His lifeless body seeped blood into the concrete of the New York street 50 stories below.

TARTAN LOUNGE

Out of the darkening Sunday afternoon sky the great winged tube hurtled. With a roar of giant Rolls Royce engines and the scuff of tires on tarmac, the tartan painted Scot Air, flight 007, from JFK touched down at Glasgow International Airport. Sarah MacEwan leaned back in her Haggis (First) Class leather chair and gave a thumbs up to the kilt-wearing steward who returned the gesture. She knew many of the employees by first name, and as Chief Technology Officer of the airline, they all knew hers.

"This is your captain again," boomed a brogue-accented voice from the intercom. "I'd like to be the first to welcome you to the United Kingdom. Please stay in your seats until we arrive at the gate and I turn off the fasten seat belt sign. Thank you for choosing our airline. We know you have a choice of carriers, but remember, if it isn't Scottish, it's crap!"

The plane taxied up to the gate, and the steward opened the door to the jetway. Sarah was the first off the plane, and nodded to the bagpipe-playing employee who stood at attention immediately outside. Moving briskly, she sailed through the Fast Track customs line. A private car was waiting which whisked her to the nearby building that currently contained both Scot Air's headquarters as well as Ian MacEwan, Founder and President of the airline - known as 'Big Mac' to many, and 'Dad' to Sarah.

His nickname was not poorly given. Ian MacEwan was a giant of a man. More than 6'3" and weighing in at 16 stone (230 lbs.), he could look positively leonine behind his bushy red shoulder-length hair and unkempt beard. Everything in his office on the top floor of the headquarters building was built to his scale: the huge office, the great bust of one artists' imagining of the Loch Ness Monster, the grand stainless steel bar with its extant assortment of single malt scotch, and the massive mahogany desk he sat behind.

"Don't forget to smile, Dad," Sarah said, as way of greeting as she walked into the office unannounced. The scowl that had pained the elder's face a moment before turned rapidly into a broad smile as he stood and hugged his only child. 5'1", slender, and with blonde hair cut short, Sarah looked positively pixie-like, and not a thing like her father. She was enveloped in his heartfelt embrace. She sat down and waited for Big Mac to do the same.

"OK, Dad, what's so important that you needed me to come all the way over from America?"

"Well, I wish I could just tell you that I had cirrhosis, but it is far worse than that. It seems that Intercontinental Air is about to announce a hostile takeover of our firm. I know we have worried about this before, but this time it seems particularly pernicious as Silverman Satchel & Co. are the lead advisors for the bid."

"But, Dad, I thought they were our advisors?"

"Yes, but the way these investment banker bastards work, they go with the money. And the fact that they are planning to back Interncontinental Air's bid, will certainly give it more credibility among our shareholders."

"It's the landing rights at Heathrow, isn't it?"

"Of course it is, lass. We knew this would happen someday."

Sarah sighed. When Scotland 'devolved' from the UK and gained its own parliament and local autonomy early in the new millennium, the senior MacEwan, had stepped into the breach by suggesting the idea of a national flag carrier – if there was a Lufthansa, an Air France and an AerLingus, why not a Scottish airline? With the help of several other ex-British Air executives, and Sir Sean Connery as honorary Chairman, he raised venture capital and launched service in 2001. The next year he was able to get Scottish members of the House of Parliament in London to force the granting of some of British Air's landing rights at Heathrow Airport to his fledgling airline. Worth more than the planes that utilized them, the landing rights were the airline's most valuable asset. The grant led to a soaring of Scot Air's share price. Unfortunately, this very access to the great hub of Heathrow made Scot Air an attractive takeover target in the consolidating world of the global airline industry.

"Alright, Dad. What's the offer going to be?"

"£3.40 a share. 30% over the current price."

"That means you can walk with more than £70 million. What's wrong with that?"

"First of all, we can grow our little cub into something worth much more than £3.40 in the next five years. And secondly – I'm not ready to retire! Golf, scotch, and playing bridge with your mother's snooty friends are not enough to fill up my days. You're my first child, but this damned airline is my second, and I'm not ready to say goodbye just yet!"

Sarah looked around the room. Her eyes were drawn to the promotional posters hanging on the walls depicting the launch of new Scot Air services:

'Bonnie lasses, hairy knees and the first round of single malt on the house,' emblazoned over a photo of a very attractive stewardess and steward in airline tartan skirt and kilt uniforms holding up bottles of Glenfidditch in front of Scot Air's first 747 at JFK airport. 'What more could you want in an airline?' read the caption below.

'Business travelers - try Scot Air's new Haggis Class,' read the text over a picture of a English businessman in traditional bowler, walrus mustache and dark pinstripe suit reclining in a sumptuous leather airline chair while being attended to by a stewardess bearing a tray of gourmet foodstuffs. 'We'll feed you till you're stuffed!'

'Introducing non-stop service from Toronto to London.' The photo below was of Ian MacEwan posing with his arm around the shoulder of actor Mike Meyers. Both wore traditional Scottish garb. One held a war mace, the other a bagpipe. 'If it's not Scottish, it's crap!' was the caption underneath.

She sighed. If Big Mac wasn't ready to give up the airline, something would have to be done. "So, Dad, what would torpedo InterContinental's bid?"

"Mmm…probably a 50% share price increase in Scot Air's stock would scare them off."

"How important is this to you."

"Sarah, I've sweated too much blood to turn this airline over to these pirates at a time not of my own choosing!"

She sat in her seat for a moment and looked out the windows as if bored. Her father had learned long ago this meant that she was actually thinking quite hard. A small smile spread across her face as the skeleton of a plan came to her. "How many laws am I allowed to break if I can get us out of this?"

Big Mac raised his eyebrows. As usual, he was impressed by his daughter. "All of them, just don't get caught."

Most airlines have special lounges for their Business and First Class customers. Scot Air was no different with its Tartan Lounge. A weary traveler entering the lounge was greeted with low decibel bagpipe music, framed photos of lonely moors, lounge chairs, a large selection of single malts, ales, soft drinks (intended as mixers), and high-speed internet service. Sarah had been the one to push the latter as the business traveler coveted by Scot Air increasingly demanded a quiet place to work and access the 'net. These businessmen used their phones and laptop computers for a great deal of personal business as well, and of course all of this personal business was 'safe' from prying eyes as it was conducted over encrypted secure servers. Of course every keystroke and viewed web page was also captured on Scot Air's Wide Area

Network (WAN) and stored on the airlines' Storage Area Network (SAN).

Sarah was looking through a glass partition at the centerpiece of the SAN, which happened to be a Symmetrix model 8730-30 server manufactured by the EMC Corporation. Sitting at a desk facing the partition was Raymond Lee, a wiry man of Korean extraction most recently from Los Angeles, who was both Scot Air's Head of Technology Operations and Sarah's current love interest. A long distance extreme kayaker who specialized in low-temperature ocean events, he was one of the few who had ever volunteered to relocate to Glasgow for the weather.

"OK pixie," he began, pointing at the CRT screen that showed output from the SAN "we're on line, and I can cull out any data you want."

"Are you sure everyone else has gone home for the weekend except the two of us?"

"Well, there might be a janitor here, but that's it…are you thinking about getting naughty at work here with me pixie? I mean, most of us want to do it on the boss' desk at some point, but hey, you are the boss – where's the excitement in that?"

Sarah gave Raymond a playful whack to the back of the head. "No, no, but what I want is very sensitive, not to mention illegal. Are you willing to help me get it, or should I just send you home too?"

"Oh, so we are hackers now are we? Now that we are finished on your desk we are just going to hack into our own firm's computers?" Raymond looked into her eyes and saw that she was serious. "Can we get a prison cell for just the two of us with matching his and hers striped uniforms?"

"Look, I want to do something for the good of the company, and I wouldn't do it if it weren't a matter of preserving its future and our jobs. I need your help as you know this system better than anyone else – I mean you were in charge of installing it. But if you can't help, just go home, and I'll try to figure it out myself. If the authorities pick up on it, I will take all the blame and state that you were never a party to this."

Raymond looked at Sarah for a brief moment before taking a deep breath, sighing, and shaking his head. "OK, I'm in. What do you want?"

"Download all activity by anyone who ever accessed a Silverman Satchel online trading account from one of our Tartan Lounge wifi servers."

7:02AM Monday morning was just a continuation of a long Sunday night for Sarah as she walked into the lobby of Silverman Satchel's headquarters' building in 'the City' of London. Not getting too close to the guards at the reception desk, she walked to the back of the building where there were three phone booths near a little tobacco shop. Sarah sat down in a booth, closed the folding glass door and pulled a laptop computer out of her shoulder bag. Plugging into the phone's data jack, loading logging into an AOL free-trial-offer account, and getting on-line took only a few moments. After that, she typed in the URL 'www.silvermanonline.com' and was directed to the brokerage site. Positioning her cursor in the data entry box asking for user name and password, Sarah activated a program cooked up with Raymond that began entering pre-typed information. There was nothing else to do but watch as her computer logged in, and then logged out over and over again, posing as more than eight hundred Silverman Satchel employees, and entering 'Buy' orders for shares of Scot Air.

After more than two and a half hours, the orders were complete, and Sarah logged off just before the laptop's battery gave out. The phone booth got a quick once-over from a pocket alcohol wipe, and she walked briskly out of the building with just a few moments left before market opening.

Lance Whittinger III, Managing Director for Mergers and Acquisitions (M&A) at Silver Satchel, was in his office early as usual. The sky was just getting light in the east when he glanced up from his desk on the 50th floor of Silverman Satchel's Midtown New York headquarters. His assistant stood in the doorway knocking lightly and then pointed to the television in the corner of the room. "Trading desk called – CNBC," was all she said before closing the door behind her. Lance picked up the remote and hit the 'On' button.

"Once again we can now confirm that Intercontinental Airlines is planning a takeover of Scot Air." Patrick Bolland, the nattily dressed CNBC announcer with the handlebar mustache, was sitting at his desk and looking into the camera. In early London trading this morning, Scot Air has been moving up steadily on big volume and is now trading at £3.45, actually, now 3.50. The stock is now up more than 25% on the day."

"Shit," said Wittinger quietly

"We can now confirm that Interncontinental Air is about to issue a press release offering to acquire all shares of Scot Air for £3.60. Traders I have spoken to tell me that this one may not go down without a fight as there may be other carriers interested in making a play here as Scot Air's landing rights at Heathrow are coveted by many carriers in both the US and Continental Europe."

"Shit," said Wittinger.- a bit more loudly this time.

"Excuse me," the assistant was back. "The CEO of Intercontinental is on the line. He seems a bit agitated."

"Great," Wittinger replied as he picked up the phone.

"Lance? What the hell is going on over there! I thought you told me that there would be no leaks." Robert Black, the head of Intercontinental Air was clearly testy and surprised, though the probability of news of a hostile takeover getting out early was always high. "I do not like receiving bad news on Monday morning before I even get my first cup of coffee down!"

"Sir, we had discussed this scenario. I cannot promise that the leak did not come from us, but I doubt you can confirm to me that it was not one of your own staff members worried about losing a job perhaps? Or how about your law firm? Those guys have big mouths built right into their DNA."

"Yeah, fine. But if I find out that someone at Silverman let this out, and it ends up costing my company money, you will find yourself working on a lot of mergers north of the Arctic Circle – don't forget that I'm a Director on Silverman's board."

"Mr. Black, you have made sure that I have never forgotten that particular point," Wittinger rolled his eyes. As if he wouldn't be at another firm in a New York Minute if they treated him poorly!

"So, Lance, what do we do now that we are in this situation that seems to be the fault of no one in particular?"

"Look, we make the offer at £3.60 as planned, and start buying shares at or below that price until you hold the maximum 9.9% allowed without clearance from the financial and competition regulators. That way, if another bidder shows up with a higher price, you either raise your bet and pay up, or you sell the shares you just bought for a nice profit. Either way you win with your Board: a bigger airline and those Heathrow slots, or a quick return on a big chunk of change."

There was silence on the other line for a moment while the CEO considered. "Lance, I'm going to authorize you to start buying that Scot Air stock up to £4 a share. We'll buy the 9.9%, but only if Silverman is willing to step in and buy 5% of the stock as well, with the understanding that you will sell it on to Intercontinental at the price you paid for it in the event that we do end up with the company. If another bidder comes along, well, then, you'll get the same great return as we will when dumping the stock."

"Mr. Black, you know that I can't authorize our trading desk to put that much of my firm's capital at risk without approval from my superiors-"

"I'm not negotiating here. Either you fax my lawyers over a written agreement or I'm walking away from this deal. Your firm will be out a big M&A fee, and you, Lance, will be out of a very large bonus. I look forward to hearing back from you in the next hour."

Wittinger found himself holding a lifeless phone receiver in his hands. This time his curse could be heard well down the hallway.

What a wonderful day it had been for Gregory Delano Howe, CEO of Silverman Satchel. With the aid of a 5mg. Ambien sleeping pill he had slept extremely well. This well deserved slumber followed a wonderful night of discussion with several friends over the future of US politics. His trophy wife, a full 27 years junior to his well-preserved 59, looked particularly ravishing at breakfast. So he ravished her. Yes, this put him a bit behind schedule, but a man has to do what a man has to do.

Alfred, Howe's driver, was still waiting patiently in front of the pre-war Park Avenue building when his charge emerged from the front door. Howe was known as 'his majesty' at the firm for his regal bearing and lifestyle: This was one of the four homes he owned (Paris, Montana, and Belize being the locations of the others). His Mercedes limousine flew two little Silverman Satchel flags on the front corners of its hood as if he were a foreign potentate being whisked across the streets of Manhattan. Dressed in the finest bespoke suit, top coat and walking stick, he rarely opened a door for himself. This fine morning was no different as he seated himself in the back of the car, and Alfred took care of the door.

It was only 18 to blocks Silverman's Headquarters, but walking was not a viable option for a man of Gregory Howe's stature. In less than ten minutes the private elevator doors opened and his majesty strode out onto the executive floor of the building. Howe almost always smiled when saw 'his' floor. The carpet was a deep cream, so plush it almost swallowed up his shoes. The walls, a dark crimson, the better to highlight the gold frames of the many old masters displayed on the walls. Old battleaxe secretaries sat behind great battleships desks restricting access to the offices of the senior executives who ran the Silverman Satchel Empire.

Howe gave a small salute to Betsy, his very own Imperial Guard, and sauntered into his office. Betsy had already printed out his most important emails (a man of Howe's stature did not keep a pedestrian computer at his desk), and he sat down at the mahogany desk to peruse to read them. All seemed to be in order, except the filing of another sexual discrimination lawsuit against Silverman by a gaggle of uppity female employees…and the rising stock price of Scot Air which could complicate its takeover by Intercontinental Air.

A butler brought in a silver service of coffee, fresh brioche, and the Wall Street Journal. Howe smiled contentedly. He thought to himself how perfect was this day: he had his health, 10% of his 17 million Silverman stock options, currently $170 million in-the-money, vested at the today's market close. And then there was his wife. She had procured a new stash of pills which were a mix of ecstasy and Viagra (she said they were called 'sexstacy' on the street). Then there was a knock at the door, and that's when the whole day started to go to hell.

"Sir, Mr. Wittinger is here" Betsy stood at the doorway. "He says that there is a problem with the Scot Air deal, and that he must speak to you immediately."

"Send him in" was the pronouncement from his majesty. The Head of M&A walked in sheepishly.

"Sir, I am sorry to bother you, but there seems that we may have a minor glitch in the Scot Air deal. I believe we are going to have to commit some of our capital towards the project." Wittinger realized he had not stopped by at an auspicious time to present his boss with bad tidings. Looking into Howe's eyes, he realized it might be a good time to update his resume'.

Fifty-five minutes later, Silverman Satchel's trading desk in London started buying large blocks of Scot Air stock.

Head equity trader, Niles Wilson, stood in the middle of a vast room of screaming traders, ringing phones, beeping computer monitors and droning computer fans. As soon as the order came through, the volume in the room had risen in pitch. Several of his minions sat around him at trading 'turrets' of mutli-line phones and searched the market for stock. None of them liked being forced to push a stock price up – an easy way to lose money – and no one was in this insane asylum for any reason other than to make money. But orders were orders, and Scot Air stock rose relentlessly up to £4. At this higher price, the Silverman traders had no problem shaking stock out of the market.

"Almost halfway there," Wilson thought to himself as he looked down at the blotter monitor on his computer. "Maybe I should have the boys ease off, and see if the price weakens?" Just then he saw on the television screen that CNBC had put up the 'Breaking News' caption and the Scot Air logo on the screen behind the anchorwoman's head. "Turn that up, now!" Wilson's bellow, and his outstretched arm and pointing finger, got the job done: the room got much quieter, and someone increased the volume until it was easily heard across the trading room.

"We now take you to Edinburgh where Ian MacEwan, President of Scot Air, is about to speak at a hastily called press conference." The anchorwoman was replaced by an image of 'Big Mac' wading up to a tartan-clad podium flanked by blue and white Scottish flags. Journalists, out of the television camera's view, snapped flash photos of the man.

"Thank you for joining me today. I have just emerged from discussions with the board this morning and believe that we speak with one voice. It is our opinion that Scot Air should not be sold and dismantled by carnivorous Yanks such as is the design of the unsolicited bid from Intercontinental Airlines to buy out our shares. It is also our opinion that the share price of Scot Air stock is significantly overvalued at its current value."

Silverman's London trading desk was suddenly very quiet. Was that actually a CEO on the television saying that his stock was too high?

"As the officers and board members of this company, it is our fiduciary duty to maximize the financial return on our corporate assets. At this time we believe that the best way to accomplish that goal is to short our own stock. As of five minutes from this announcement, our treasury department will use most of our free cash balances to buy Put options on our stock. Thank you for your attention. I will be taking no questions at this time." MacEwan walked away from the podium and left the room under a hail of shouted questions from the press.

"Holy crap!" yelled out one of the equity traders. "He just called down an airstrike on his own position! Can he even do that?" he asked his boss.

For the first time at work in many years, Wilson was stunned. All he could do was shrug. Then he picked up the phone and called the head office in New York.

"I am going to chew your ass down to a bloody little pulp, Lance!" Mr. Black was not happy and all trace of the aloof Airline CEO was gone. He had started out as a spoiled little bully at a spoiled little prep school in Massachusetts, and all the meanness from his youth was crackling across the phone line.

"Yes, sir, Mr. Black. Look, no one has ever done this before according to our lawyers. We aren't even sure yet if it is legal, but there just may not be any rule barring Scot Air's actions. I don't see how it causes any significant complication to your plans though." Wittinger held up his hands and looked across the room at his boss.

"What are you smoking over there! The stock is already down 10% since that blowhard, MacEwan, made his idiotic announcement. Tell me again why we are paying you fools over at Silverman a 1% fee on a £1 billion deal?

"Mr. Black, I am sure-"

"Robert," Howe, a prep school class mate of the Interncontinental CEO, stepped up to the speakerphone and interrupted. "Clearly these Scots have decided to fight. We knew that this was an eventuality. I suggest we do the following: finish buying the shares that we already agreed to acquire, and then file suit as shareholders against MacEwan and the Scot Air Board for breach of fiduciary duty – after all, we are shareholders now and I can't see how using company cash to buy puts on one's own stock is a good use of funds. Then we will be in the plaintiff's' position, and we can try to set up a meeting with them tomorrow to discuss a compromise. I personally guarantee you that if this deal ends up being more expensive than our initial range of expectations, we will handle your follow-on bond offering at ½ the usual fee."

"Alright, Gregory. This sounds like just another way for you guys to squeeze extra cash out of me and protect your fee, but I will take your word that you can settle this for us quickly. See if you can set up the meeting. Good bye." Wittinger pushed the button to hang up the speaker phone and looked up at his boss, who was not smiling. Betsy knocked at the door, and the day took another turn for the worse.

"Sir, Mrs. Bertrand is outside, and she is clearly upset."

Joan Bertrand, Silverman's CFO was clearly upset. She strode into the room and slammed the door. And at 294 lbs., she could really slam a door.

"Greg, we've got a real freakin' problem here!

"Yes, Joan. I realize that the Scot Air deal has become …complicated, and that we have one of our own board members, in the person of Mr. Black, quite irritated."

"No, Greg," replied Bertrand, "it's a lot worse than that! It seems a few of our SilvermanOnline accounts have been compromised – someone stole the access passwords to the accounts of at least 750 of our own employees and logged in this morning and placed buy orders for guess which stock?"

Lance Wittinger sat down in one of the office's overstuffed chairs and began thinking about the best font for his resume.

"Scot Air?" asked Howe incredulously.

"Bingo! Our own employees, or at least their accounts bought almost £100 million in Scot Air stock early this morning – now worth £125 million – quite a quick and tidy profit I might add."

The phone, which Wittinger wore in a holster on his belt was set on 'vibrate'. The whole time he had been in Howe's office, it had buzzed every few minutes as a new email or text arrived. Of course, he had not dared check their import while in his boss' presence. But now the little device began to buzz constantly. Someone was sending him a message every second. Hesitantly he reached down to his hip and read the list of identical messages on the screen – "TURN ON CNBC! SCOT AIR IN TROUBLE – WILSON"

"And Greg, it gets worse than that," continued the CFO.

"Worse?"

"I think we should turn on the television," Wittinger suggested.

"Again, it seems as if what goes up must go down," said Pat Bolland with a smile. What CNBC commentator doesn't love a good story to keep the ratings strong? "The rumors are all over the internet stock chat boards – that Scot Air bet a significant portion of its equity capital in aviation fuel derivatives late last year in an attempt to lock in a set level of operating costs. Now it seems, according to these rumors, that these derivative bets have gone horribly wrong, and the company is close to having to declare bankruptcy. Scot Air's response to clarification was simply, 'the company does not comment on market rumors' While these rumors may not have been substantiated, they have been enough to send Scot Air's stock down to just a bit over £3 a share in the last 15 minutes. What a crazy ride!"

"Sir," Betsy hesitantly poked her head in through a crack in the door. "I've got Mr. Black on line one . He claims that he must speak to you immediately-"

"I'm not here right now!" Howe shouted angrily.

"And Mr. Arthur Tivel on line two who claims that he must speak to you immediately"

Howe begrudgingly picked up the phone. Even Gregory Delano Howe did not dodge a direct call from the Chairman of the SEC.

"Arthur. Good to hear from you. Is there any way I could call you back tomorrow?"

"Only if you think I should just ignore the report one of my people just gave me. It seems to indicate that a whole bunch of your people bought Scot Air stock just before it was announced that Intercontinental Air, under your firm's advisory, was making a bid for the company."

"Oh, yes, there is that. We just found out about that. It seems that someone compromised our system and entered these trades just to make us look bad. I'm going to have Joan Bertrand, our CFO, call your office back in five minutes to fill you in on what we know. I assure you, Silverman Satchel will offer all assistance in this matter, and we are very much interested in the apprehension of these hackers who have attempted to besmirch the reputation of this fine firm. Ah…Arthur, would you mind holding on a moment?" Still holding the phone receiver in his hand, Howe turned to focus on the television set which seemed to have suddenly become much more interesting to both Bertrand and Wittinger.

"This Scot Air…it just gets stranger by the minute." Pat Bolland shook his head. "We have now confirmed what has started showing up in internet stock chatrooms a few moments ago. Historically, Scot Air does not, repeat, does not, have a policy about not commenting on market rumors. In fact, management has often commented on the validity of

128

rumors in the past. Fairly or not, this is being viewed as confirmation that the aviation fuel derivative rumors were valid, and the stock is now trading at £2.73.

Robert Black, CEO of Intercontinental Air, was furious. As a squash player back at prep school he was famous for breaking his racquet (always an expensive one at that) against the floor whenever he lost a match. Now, no racquet on hand, a yard-long scale model of InterContinental's' new Airbus Superjumbojet flew through the air and smashed against the wall. At least there were more where that one came from: Black's giant Chicago office was a veritable airplane model showroom. Every plane type flown by Interncontinental was represented here from the earliest DC-3 to the current Boeing 787. Reflective for a moment, Black mused that he had never really liked the new giant Airbus anyway. In two quick strides he reached the remains of the shattered plastic fuselage, and gave it a swift kick that launched it back across the room. He picked up the phone and hit 'redial'. Howe was not going to get away with a secretary holding him at arms' length!

"Mr. Howe's office."

"This is Robert Black calling again. I demand to speak to Mr. Howe immediately!"

There was a pause, and then Howe came onto the line, "Hello, Robert. I'm sorry I could not take your call earlier." He sounded…unusual. As if there was something about which he was quite embarrassed.

"I'm pretty pissed off here. This deal has gone to hell on us, and now I've got to explain to my board how Intercontinental lost a bundle trading Scot Air stock today. Of course, you will have to explain to your board, meaning me, among others, how Silverman Satchel could mess anything up as badly as this!"

"Robert-"

"Don't interrupt me – I'm your client. You will listen to me even if you think your shit doesn't stink and you act like nobility! First of all, sell every one of InterContinental's shares of Scot Air. Now!"

There was a pause, and Black could hear some muted conversation on the other side of the line. "All right, Robert. I think it is a bad idea, but we will begin selling the stock immediately."

"Very good. Next, I am having my PR department put out a release that we are dropping our bid for Scot Air. And don't think Silverman Satchel will be getting one red cent out of Interncontinental for your 'work' on this deal."

Howe sighed loudly. "Fine, Robert. I am sorry that everything turned out so badly. However, I hope you understand that this unfortunate turn of events was not necessarily the fault of my firm. Clearly there was a nefarious actor involved here. Someone stole a great number of my employees' access codes to our online brokerage system and bought significant sums of Scot Air stock this morning. As you can imagine, the SEC is quite interested in how this could happen."

"And how does this concern me?" asked the CEO of Intercontinental testily.

"Well, our tech people have been able to trace all of these unauthorized trades to a single internet session in London from a phone booth in the ground floor of our building. The caller used a newly opened America Online account, and that firm tells us that the account was registered under the name Robert Black."

"You aren't implying that I had anything to do with this?"

"Well, the credit card used to open the account at America Online was your corporate American Express Card. I am certainly not saying that you were involved Robert. But I do want to warn you, that after we turn this information over to the SEC, it is quite likely they will want to speak to you."

Back in Chicago, a plastic model of an Intercontinental Air Boeing 787 flew gracefully through the air and impacted in a shatter of plastic against the far wall.

Big Mac held up a bottle of single malt and clinked it against his daughter's glass. "Sarah, you are brilliant – just brilliant." He held the bottle up to his lips and took a long pull. Sarah downed her glass with a flourish and held it out for more.

Refilling the glass, the big man asked, "What I don't understand is how you were able to get your hands on that bastard Black's Amex card?"

"Oh, I never had the card Dad. It's just that late last year, Mr. Black was flying back to Chicago from London. The Intercontinental flight he was supposed to take was delayed five hours due to a problem with the landing gear, so we gave him a seat on our afternoon non-stop. Of course, his credit card number was saved in our computers when he bought something from the on-board duty free cart."

Big Mac roared with laughter at that. He raised his bottle in another toast, crashed it dangerously hard against Sarah's glass. "Here's to Scot Air – the airline with the best on time record in the British Isles!" They both drank with gusto to that.

"After all this, Dad, I hope you will be slowing down soon to let me take over the reins?"

"Oh, a couple more years of fun, and then I'll let you kick me upstairs to the Chairmanship and you can call the shots. But for now," a wicked gleam came into his eyes, "I'm still your boss." They both laughed as he tousled her hair with his free hand. "Well, my child. Let's wrap this up." Adjusting his tie, and handing the bottle to Sarah, Big Mac walked through the door of his office and down the hall to the conference room where the press had been summoned for the second time that day.

Sarah watched the proceedings on the large screen television in the office. The podium barely concealed Big Mac's girth.

"Ladies and gentlemen, it is the opinion of the Management and Board of Directors of Scot Air that our stock is no longer overvalued. In fact, it is now in our opinion, undervalued. We have been closing out our put positions on the stock – all of which are in the black, I might add. The Board has also authorized the management of Scot Air to utilize cash proceeds on our balance sheet to repurchase our own shares in the open market. These purchases will begin immediately, and are expected to result in a significant increase in the price of our shares. We welcome the withdrawal of Interncontinental Air's bid for our airline. We believe our shareholders will be best rewarded through Scot Air's continued independence. I am afraid I will take no questions at this time. Thank you."

There was a muted roar behind Sarah, and she turned to the window to see the tartan painted Scot Air, flight 008, taking off from the Glasgow Airport enroute to JFK. She poured another shot, and held up her glass towards the plane.

"Fly free," she said in way of a toast. "At least until I decide to sell you off for scrap."

SMALL CAP

With the stroke of a pen it was done, and sitting in Seattle, Jonah Grant, portfolio manager of the Kingpin Aging Demographics Fund, hung his head. All around him others were doing the same, and suffering in silence except those few who actually let out a groan or a whimper. Then, for a moment, there was complete silence in the room and the seated audience sat still in front of the video conference hook-up before them.

When Jonah returned his gaze to the giant video screen beaming in images from New York, the picture displayed Walter Jones, CEO of OKunlimited Capital Management, Ltd. beaming broadly and pumping the hand of Kenichi Toda, CEO of Kingpin Wasabi Asset Management who was bravely attempting to retain his dignity in the presence of such emotion. Behind the two luminaries stood a score of investment banker, lawyer and corporate drones wearing wool suits and polyester smiles.

For five years Jonah had worked for Kingpin and built a successful career as one of its portfolio managers. But, now that OKunlimited had bought the company from its crippled Japanese bank owners, what was the future to bring? The entire Kingpin office staff had been called into the video conference room to view the signing, and Jonah was not the only one who felt the cold hand of unemployment on his wallet.

The management of both OKunlimited and Wasabi Bank had done their best to spin the news of the sale as a great one for everyone: OKunlimited, Wasabi, fund shareholders, and Kingpin. But Jonah, and his fellow employees knew that acquisitions rarely went well, and what was the future of an employee in Seattle, working for a company based in Tulsa?

After a few moments of warmed-over revenue synergy speech from Walter Jones, Jonah got up and walked out of the conference room and strode down the long, lushly-

133

carpeted hallway to his office. On his way, he heard a sound come from the apparently empty office of Peter Monroe, portfolio manager of the Kingpin Global Gimmick Portfolio. He stepped in and listened. There it was again - a slurping sound Jonah stepped further into the office, looked around, and then down. He was surprised to see Peter staring up at him from under the desk, where he was reading an annual report and drinking from a can of Diet Dr. Pepper.

"Want some?" Peter asked offering the can. "It's not just for breakfast anymore."

"No, thanks. You comfortable down there?"

"Yeah, well," Peter clambered to his feet, as Jonah stepped back. "I had very little interest in watching Toda sign away the family jewels." Peter sat down in the large leather chair behind the desk, and Jonah lowered himself into the plush couch in front of it. These were the very positions where the two spent many an hour each day. "Anyway," Peter continued. "I was afraid that Joan of Arc would insist on my attendance, as the stupid memo did say that the videoconference was 'mandatory' for all personnel".

As if on cue, Trish Abut stuck her head into the office. Peter and Jonah's assistant was known for being, punctilious and keeping everyone else in line. It was not always clear who worked for whom.

"I didn't see you at the teleconference" she stated - an accusation.

"I was ... at the back of the room'" Peter lied lamely. Trish muttered something under her breath and disappeared down the hallway.

Both men chuckled softly. While great friends, they probably could not have been more dissimilar: Physically, Peter was thin and wiry, while Jonah was beefy and built like an undersized linebacker. Peter was quiet and confident, Jonah was brash and prone to let his insecurities show.

134

However, both had made it through several restructurings at Kingpin, and moved up the ranks together, to a point where they managed their mutual funds with a great deal of autonomy from the firm's head offices in New York and Osaka.

"So, what comes next? Is it time for us to put our reorg boots on again?"

"No, Peter, I think this time we are going to need wings to keep above the bullshit. OKunlimited doesn't really need any of us'"

Peter pulled out a pack of cigarettes, turned on an air purifier, lit up and inhaled deeply. "Well, in that case, I guess I won't have to worry about breaking the rules anymore" He exhaled a large cloud of smoke in the direction of the 'No Smoking - California Law' sign which Trish had mounted above the door a year earlier.

One thing could certainly be said about OKunlimited – they worked fast. Only a few days after the September rumors appeared in the press that Kingpin was for sale, OKuntimited announced its intention to buy. A remarkably short two weeks later - clearly to the consternation of the consultants and lawyers involved, who charged by the hour - the deal had been consummated. And now, only two days after that, Gerald Gain, Chief Investment Officer of OK Funds was sitting in Peter Monroe's office. With a net worth in excess of $400 million, he had been one·of the founders of OK Capital Management in the mid-1980s. OK's earning momentum-style funds had performed brilliantly in a long bull market and Gain enjoyed a commensurate rise in wealth. This value was realized when OK merged with Unlimited Asset Management Ltd of London in late 1999 to form the improbable name of the new corporate holding company.

"I understand that you may be a bit concerned Peter, so I'm just going to talk turkey with you," Gain drawled. "We've looked over your portfolio; we like the performance numbers you have generated for that Gimmick Fund of yours and we could really use you down in Tulsa."

"I appreciate your confidence in my abilities Mr. Gain."

"GG, please."

"Ah, O.K. ... GG. But any possibility of me staying here in Seattle?"

"Look, I'd rather you not let this get around right away until we have a chance to talk to everyone - but this office is closing down."

"You don't plan to move 450 people to Tulsa, do you?"

"Nope, just a few key employees who are willing to embrace change and move to a great city where the cost of living is low, and who will get an opportunity to work for a fantastic company that has gone from strength to strength."

There followed an uncomfortable silence. Finally, Peter cleared his throat.

"What are you offering?"

"Well, your fund's name will switch from Kingpin to OK. You get the same salary you have now. We will pay your moving expenses, of course. And you will be reviewed for inclusion in our partnership program in the near future."

"I'm sorry to ask this, but if I decide not to move?"

"Well, we'd be real sorry to lose you. But in a couple of months, at the end of this year, your employment would be ... terminated, I believe, is the term the lawyers currently use, and you would get two weeks of severance for each year you have worked for Kingpin. Your funds would be transferred to one of our managers in Tulsa, and you would be free to move on to any other employer that suits you."

"Is it all right with you if I think this over for a few days? I mean, it is a pretty big decision."

"Peter," Gain let slip a huge genuine smile as he stood up and slapped Peter on the shoulder. "Take your time. You come on down to Tulsa and visit with the whole posse of us at OK. I have no doubt that you will want to join us." He put out his hand and shook with Peter. "I'm afraid I have to move on to my next meeting, but you give me a call if-you have any questions."

A moment later and Peter was alone in his office.

He stared out the window at the Seattle skyline which was currently besieged by a monstrous rope of fog moving in off the Puget Sound. There was a knock on the doorframe.

"So, Pete. You get the big offer to head over to London?

Monroe turned his chair around to look at Jonah, who was already lowering himself into the couch. "No, they said I have to go to Tulsa. You got London?"

"Yeah, but I lose my independent Portfolio Manager position. I have to be part of the Unlimited Health Sciences team. My assigned role is to follow the big, boring, European pharmaceutical firms. No way am I doing that. Similar to sex, Portfolio Management is not as much fun as a team sport.» Both men laughed at that, and then Jonah asked a one word question, "Tulsa?"

"You mean would I move to Oklahoma where the sheep are nervous, and the women even more nervous? No frigin' way am I going there. I'd rather take the severance package and go do something else."

"Any interest in making that package a little bit bigger?" Jonah asked with a mischievous grin.

"What do you have in mind?"

Earnings momentum equity investing as practiced in the final days of the 20th century by OKunlimited and a score of other large institutional investors was quite simple and worked wonderfully in roaring bull markets:

Premise #1: stocks trade on earnings, and the higher the earnings, the higher the stock price.

Premise #2: backtested statistics from the 1970s through the 1990s showed that earnings surprises were linearly correlated - in other words, if a company reported better than expected earnings one quarter, it had a better than 50% chance of reporting another positive earnings surprise the next quarter.

Premise #3: Analysts working for the large investment banks are by nature conservative in their earnings estimates. A result of this is that, when analysts increase their expected earnings forecast for a company, that company has a better than 50% statistical expectation of reporting earnings that are in excess of those analysts' consensus expectations.

Earnings momentum had allowed OKunlimited to develop a business with more than a trillion dollars under management generating revenues in excess of three billion dollars a year. They managed open-ended mutual funds that did just one thing: Purchase stocks that exhibited recent earnings surprises and were lucky enough to have had their earnings outlook upgraded by Wall Street.

However, any system can be manipulated - especially the simple ones. And in the case of OKunlimited's assumption of control of the Kingpin funds, Jonah and Peter had been handed an awesome opportunity to make money, as long as they were willing to forgo all sense of fiduciary responsibility and place their personal financial interests ahead of those of their fund's shareholders. For a month they did little that would have been noticeable to OKunlimited even if it had been checking. That the two friends traveled with a couple of girlfriends to Caribbean islands that happened to have strict banking secrecy laws was not all that out of the ordinary. Neither was a slight increase in the number of trades in the accounts that the two Portfolio Managers controlled.

Slowly but surely, Peter and Jonah liquidated the larger market capitalization stocks in the Global Gimmick Portfolio and Aging Demographics Fund with histories of earnings surprises and recent earnings upgrades. The cash freed from these liquid, blue-chip names was invested in small companies that just happened to have disappointed the Street in recent quarters by reporting lower than expected earnings. Gradually, as the year wound down, the two portfolios came to resemble more and more, small cap, value-oriented equity funds.

"Three, two, one!" screamed the crowd at the bar.

With a synchronized popping of champagne corks by the three bartenders, the year 2001 came to an end. Jonah kissed Kim, his girlfriend of six months. Peter, who had been dumped by his girlfriend in November and arrived at the bar stag, appeared quite happy as he kissed the Virgin America flight attendant (Lisa? Leslie?) that he had just met an hour before.

"O.K., I'm definitely drunk," Jonah declared. "Someone get me another drink!"

"Round's on me," Peter replied as he attempted to brush glittering confetti out of his hair that the stewardess had just thrown on him.

"Hold on, 1 think you got the last two. Let me pay for one," she interjected.

"Oh, that's O.K., Lisa," she didn't look hurt, so he must have gotten the name right. "I just got fired , so all the rounds are on me."

"Oh, Peter, that's awful," Lisa exclaimed, genuinely concerned. Both Peter and Jonah reacted by laughing drunkenly.

139

"Don't worry," Jonah slurred, as he leaned against Kim and threw his arm over her shoulder. "Getting fired is going to be the most lucrative thing that has ever happened to him!" Peter glared at his friend, but Jonah didn't stop. "We are going to teach those asses over at OKunlimited not to mess with us."

Further down the bar, Greg Nusan, Field Examiner Grade XII, at the Federal Reserve Bank of San Francisco, caught wind of the Portfolio Manager's drunken boast with interest. While the Fed did not have jurisdiction over the regulation of mutual fund companies, he often worked alongside his counterparts from the SEC. Nusan pulled out his phone and jotted a note to himself to make a call on January 2nd - or whenever the hangover he was earning tonight raged down. Putting the phone back in his pocket, he returned his attention to his beer and noisemaker.

On Monday, the second of January, Jonah and Peter both arrived at Kingpin's offices to pick up their severance checks, and say a final goodbye to those who had not yet been let go by OKunlimited. One of their last duties before heading out to the beach was to sign the required forms relinquishing their trading responsibility over the accounts they had managed until so very recently. Meanwhile, in Tulsa, Gerald Gain heard a knock at the door to his office.

"Come in," he ordered, and in walked Darren Jordan, one of OK's jack-of-all-trades Portfolio Managers. University of Chicago MBA trained, with a focus on economic statistics, he carried a large stack of his trademark quantitative reports, and placed two of them in front of Gain before speaking.

"Sorry to bother you GO, but I think we have a bit of a problem with two of the accounts we just took over from Kingpin. Specifically, Aging Demographics and Global Gimmick." He waited patiently and adjusted the thick glasses on his nose as his boss scanned over the sheets of numbers.

"The bastards!" roared Gain.

"I take it you didn't know about this?"

"Damn straight, I didn't! When I looked at these two portfolios a couple of months ago they looked pretty good to me. Not perfect OK Fund portfolios of course, but good enough and the performance numbers were just fine. Now look at the things! They are filled with crap. 1 don't see a stock with a market cap over $500 million in here, and many of them have recently missed their earnings."

"Ah, GG, they have all missed their numbers, they all have had estimates slashed, and all have had their stocks hit as a result. If we want to run these portfolios with our discipline, we will have to sell every single holding. I estimate that the funds will each take a 3-10% hit to performance just in commission and spread costs alone. And then there is the chance that prices will gap down as we try to unload such large holdings.

"Well, we don't have much choice do we? Do it, but do it quietly - the less the Street knows that we are unloading these small cap stocks, the better - not to mention the potential embarrassment to the firm. Tell me when you're done though, because then we are going to skewer the bastards."

The next day, Gain was disturbed by his secretary, who informed him that there was a field agent from the SEC on the phone. OKunlimited ran a clean shop, and exams by the regulators were routine. Even so, he pushed the button on his speakerphone with some level of trepidation.

"Gain here."

"Mr. Gain. This is Agent Malm from the SEC in New York. I am calling about two of your portfolio managers - Monroe and Grant" Gain's hands clenched themselves into fists. "We have heard a rumor that they may be engaged in some inappropriate behavior."

"Mr. Monroe and Mr. Grant no longer work for the firm, and we no longer have any professional relationship with them."

"Even so, Mr. Gain, I would like to send a small team out to your offices later this week to look over their personal trading records and the portfolios that they manage, excuse me, managed for you.

"Of course," Gain struggled to keep his voice calm. "Let me put you through to our legal department and they will work out all the details. Call me back if you have any difficulty. Hold on a moment." Gain dialed in the legal department's extension, hit the 'transfer' button and then swore loudly at the top of his lungs. In the hallway outside of Gain's office, workers stopped in their tracks for a moment, and then hurried away from the vicinity ¬no one wanted to be near the boss when he was that angry.

Gain next called up Kathy Liek in Accounts Payable. "Kathy, quick question for you. Is there any chance we can put a stop order on the severance checks we issued to two of the Kingpin employees, Monroe and Grant?"

There was the sound of computer keys being clicked. "I'm sorry GO, but those checks were already cashed. Monroe and Grant must have gone straight to the bank."

By the fourth of January, Jonah and Peter were starting to make money, and as the days progressed, the pace of their trading profits began to increase significantly . They had placed most of their assets in their offshore trading accounts, and then shorted almost all of the small cap stocks that they had so recently bought for their mutual funds. As OK began to sell these very same small company stocks to be replaced with larger companies exhibiting earnings momentum characteristics, the prices of the smaller cap stocks came under pressure and began to gap down. Like a lobster that finds it easy to crawl into a trap, but then cannot figure out how to get out - it is almost always easier to buy a small cap stock than to sell it - especially when the Street has gotten wind that there is a big seller out there. And unfortunately for OKunlimited, the Street soon knew way too much.

At 9AM on January fifth, the sun was burning brightly across the plains of Tulsa. James Rasner, senior consul for OKunlimited, drove to work as usual, but his mind was troubled. He had spent much of the day before preparing information for the SEC examiners who were due to descend on his firm that morning. It seemed that they had only one interest: the investigation of Misters Grant and Monroe. And what targets they were! While it was unclear that the two ex-portfolio managers had broken the law, they had clearly violated their fiduciary responsibility. They knew that loading up their portfolios with small cap stocks would lead to a complete and expensive repositioning of holdings upon assumption of control by OKunlimited. Monroe and Grant would be lucky to get off with just a ban on employment in the US financial industry.

But this is not what troubled Rasner at the moment.

He was thinking about the $500,000 worth of OKunlimited stock options which were to be awarded to him on the 15th of the month. The lower the company's share price on that day, the more he stood to garner in the next five years. What if the press happened to find out about Monroe and Grant? Regulatory uncertainty was sure to make the stock fall for a day or so, but as the company was clearly not at fault here, the shares would likely recover quickly. No harm done, right? Right. Now that he had explained away the morality of his greed, Rasner pulled his car over to a 'Circle K' convenience store. He used the last remaining payphone at a Circle K store to call a friend who worked in New York at a particular newspaper. Rasner's information came with one caveat - it could not break until Monday of the next week - after all, the SEC needed time to have potentially 'leaked' the information themselves.

143

On January ninth the Wall Street Journal carried a short but pointed article on page C4:

New York- OKunlimited Portfolio Managers Under SEC Investigation for Potential Mishandling of Shareholder Funds. Informed sources report that Mr. Peter Monroe, former Portfolio Manager of the OK Global Gimmick Fund and Mr. Jonah Grant, former Portfolio Manager of the OK Aging Demographics Fund are under investigation by the Security and Exchange Commission Division for allegedly violating their fiduciary responsibility to fund shareholders. The two managers were relieved of their positions soon after the OK Fund's parent company, OKunlimited Capital Management Ltd, acquired their former employer, Kingpin Wasabi Asset Management. The SEC is investigating whether or not the composition of the portfolios was intentionally reallocated with smaller capitalization stocks in advance of the change of control with the portfolio managers' foreknowledge that OKunlimited would sell smaller holdings resulting in excess trading and turnover costs for fund shareholders.

OKunlimited declined to comment on the matter, and a spokesperson/or the SEC would only say that examinations of US mutual fund companies were regular and routine. Mr. Grant, reached in Seattle, denied any wrongdoing. "I cannot speak for my former colleague, Mr. Monroe, but it is my opinion that smaller cap stocks are a much better value at this time then their larger brethren. The fund's prospectus placed no limits on the market capitalization of the portfolio's holdings, specifying only that those holdings be publically traded and oriented to take advantage of aging demographics in the US and overseas. If OKunlimited wishes to change the orientation of the fund now that they have been approved as its investment advisor that is not my concern, though I certainly think it should be one for the fund's shareholders."

All across the financial community, traders, portfolio managers, investment bankers and speculators turned to their Bloomberg or Reuters information terminals and called up the holdings of the OK Aging Demographics Fund and the OK Global Gimmick Fund. Data for both was current as of the end of December, and all the stocks on the list had bulls-eyes suddenly painted on them. Those who knew how OKunlimited managed funds, and many who did not in the morning, did by the afternoon, immediately steered clear of, or even shorted, those stocks. By the end of the trading day Daren Jordan warily made his way into Gerald Gain's office.

"Boss, I'm afraid the damage to both of the portfolios today was significant. Global Gimmick was down by 15%, and Aging Demographics was off by 21 %. That article in the Journal just killed us. We weren't even able to get a bid in for some of the stocks, with our intentions hanging out there in the wind."

"How much of the junk had you moved in the last few days?" Gain asked with a growl.

"Only about 20% of the portfolios has been turned over. You told me to do it quietly, and I had no idea that the news was going to get out -"

"Don't worry, Daren, it's not your fault. But damn, when I find out who leaked this story, I am going to stick his head in a blender! I imagine you have noticed that our stock was down $5 today. That's more than $1 billion dollars in market capitalization wiped out by some idiot with a big mouth. Now I've got to go and explain the situation to the Board, and they aren't going to be very happy about suddenly finding their options losing value."

"Any idea who called the Journal, GG?"

"None at all. It could have been anyone - the SEC, one of our own people," Gain paused for a moment. "It could have even been Monroe or Grant "

145

Three days later, Grant and Monroe closed out their short positions and were close to $12 million dollars richer, but no longer living in the United States. Things had gotten just a bit too hot for them in Seattle, and they decided that it was time to move on to safer pastures. Luckily, Vietnam did not yet have an extradition treaty with the United States, and American Airlines was more than happy to fly them there. Jonah had already decided how to spend his ill-gotten wealth. With no better ideas, Peter had gone along for the ride. Within a week, the two had purchased a small island 25 miles northeast of Haiphong. The world's newest eco-tour resort was soon to be born.

It was amazing what a little money could do in the right part of the world. Within six weeks, ten rustic bungalows had been built along the water for the soon to arrive guests. An absence of telephones, radios and television was one of the primary selling points for those wealthy patrons who really needed to get away from it all. A couple of Siberian tigers, illegally imported from China, and placed in a large moated compound, were to be the big draw. With twice daily feedings of live goats, rabbits, and the occasional water buffalo, there was little doubt that the average millionaire from Hong Kong would be interested in the show.

And for the children, well there was no shortage of aging tame dolphins from aquariums around the world no longer energetic enough to put on a prime-time show. After stringing a net and floating fence across the entrance of another of the island's lagoons, the four purchased aquatic mammals were there to stay - eager to swim with the guests as long as there was a supply of fresh fish to be fed to them.

What about the wives of these wealthy guests?

The new resort proprietors were at a loss until Peter remembered a woman he had met in Ho Chi Minh City earlier in their trip who was, among other skills, a very good masseuse. It was not long before her full-time services were obtained to perform spa, massage and aromatherapy for the guests.

Only a couple of hundred air miles from Guangzhou and Hong Kong, the new 'Green Emerald Island Resort' received its first two helicopter-loads of guests at the end of March. A glowing review appeared in the South China Daily News by a reporter who had graciously accepted an all-expenses paid trip, and soon, the resort was fully booked through September.

The two former portfolio managers continued to monitor the markets and trade their portfolios with the assistance of the Bloomberg terminals installed in their quarters, which, like those of the guests, were equipped with high-speed Internet access, satellite television, waterbeds and stereos.

In one of those inexplicable acts of the global financial markets, the first quarter of 2002 saw an underperformance of the share prices of large blue chip stocks in the U.S while the price of smaller issues rose. Thus, Peter and Jonah's 'bet' on small vs. large cap stocks was substantially validated. This took much of the wind out of the sails of the SEC's regulatory complaint which had been filed in a Federal court against the two former portfolio managers. By late April, a legal compromise had been- worked out - if both Peter and Jonah paid a $200,000 fine, and remained outside the U.S. securities industry for a full year, the SEC would drop the complaint. The accused would not have to admit to any wrongdoing. There was the IRS who wanted to perform an audit, but that was the purpose of off-shore numbered accounts in Caribbean islands.

Jonah and Peter accepted the agreement with the SEC, and emailed instructions to their lawyers in New York to transfer funds to pay the fines. Leaving their bungalows, they walked down to the helipad to receive the next installment of guests. As they arrived, a waiter presented them with their customary tropical drinks, complete with tiny parasols.

The helicopter landed and the doors were opened.

As the passengers disembarked, young women ran up and placed leis of fragrant flowers around their necks. Others offered drinks to the guests. The two proprietors greeted each new arrival personally. It was a good day.

KNOWLEDGE WORKERS

Gazing upon the promised land is not much fun when the view is obstructed by a twelve foot high electrified fence. Deion Sanders Washington unfortunately stood on the wrong side of that barrier as he looked up at the lights of Yerba Buena's Pacific Heights neighborhood. After a moment's reflection, the solidly-built young man turned his attention back to the business at hand. He was at the corner of Golden Gate and Laguna, an area known as the Mart.

The gray steel and barbed wire of the Fortified Zone along Geary Street was only yards away from one of the purest areas of capitalism in San Francisco. Men and women of every race, creed and personal armament wandered through the neighborhood selling anything proscribed by the government of the United States of America. SFPD, undermanned, underarmed and underpaid avoided the area. Besides, police operations so close to the Fortified Zone would be in danger of starting a firefight with the Marines dug in along the northern side of the barrier.

Thanks to smart-virus pigmentation caplets, Deion's skin was as black as a moonless night sky. In clothing of a similar hue, he was almost invisible against the cityscape. However, many of the proprietors and patrons of the Mart wore Doppler-sights over one eye allowing them to determine from a distance, what was shadow and what was not. Deion quickly identified the woman he was looking for and greeted her with both empty hands in view.

"Yo Roxanne. you happy to see me?"

The well proportioned woman eyed Deion with narrowed eyes. A bodyguard stood only a few feet away, the large and ugly muzzle of his pulse-rifle pointed at Deion's feet.

"Only if you have the cash."

The dark figure slowly reached inside his ankle-length leather coat and produced a plastic value card. Roxanne took it from him cautiously and slipped it through the reader of her e-purse. An eleven digit number glowed a soft red in the darkened street. "It's all there lady. Twenty billion Yuan. Don't worry. My organization never lets a supplier down."

"Whatev," she replied while making a small carefree motion with her hand. A second bodyguard emerged from between two burned out Victorian style homes and handed Deion a black plastic briefcase.

"Nice doing business with you. Don't spend it all in one place." With a vividly white smile he turned and began to walk away.

"Don't you want to check it?"

Deion stopped for a moment and turned halfway around. "No. I'm sure it's all there. Just next time, spring for a leather case, all right. This thing is tacky. At least you got the color right." In a moment, Deion was only visible to Roxanne by Doppler-sight, and after an initial flash of anger, Roxanne chuckled quietly and shook her head.

Vishali Sing was awakened from her nap by the soft, insistent pulsing emanating from her wrist computer. She sat up in bed and looked out the large picture window before her. On a clear night like this one, the great sweep of Pacific Heights, the San Francisco Bay and the Golden Gate Dam presented an awesome sight. The lithe young woman climbed out of bed and moved towards the bathroom. Still wiping sleep out of her eyes she made a quick clicking sound in her mouth to activate the computer interface before saying softly, "Lights, all, medium." Immediately the one-bedroom apartment was bathed in soft light. Vishali stood at the sink and after washing her face, began applying her eye makeup.

A toneless voice emanated from the wrist computer, "Incoming call. Lisa Ye, sender"

[click] Outgoing voice only," Vishali replied. A dim red laser shot out from her wrist and quickly found the small LCD panel mounted on the wall above the vanity. Lisa's smiling face appeared there. The laser continued to lock onto the panel even as the wrist-based computer unit shifted with its wearer

"Hey Vish," she greeted. Then noticing the lack of return image, continued, "Is it that bad?"

"Yeah, well I just woke up and I was afraid that Jim might be around."

"Nope, we are devoid of life over here. But he is on his way over." Lisa pulled back from her LCD screen to display the rest of her living room.

Knotting a silk robe around her waist Vishali once again spoke to her wrist computer, "[click] outgoing image." Instantly the LCD's viewer-on light began blinking and a second red laser lanced out of the panel to intercept the wrist computer. "So what's up for tonight?"

"Well a bunch of us are meeting at The Dive at nine. You better be there, and...I wouldn't wear that robe, you might set a trend."

Vishali smiled, "Don't worry, I'll change. What are you wearing?

"Oh, the regular. High Victorian collar, ankle length skirt, no nonsense shoes." Both women laughed as Lisa did not own a skirt that reached her knees, much less her ankles.

"Well, if you've got it, flaunt it. I guess you have to make sure you keep Jim's attention."

"Oh, don't worry Vish. One look in the wrong direction, and he'll be on the couch for a week."

"At 'a girl. I'll see you in an hour or so, o.k.? Thanks for calling. [click] End call."

The lasers vanished and the LCD panel went blank. Vishali walked over to her closet and began to look for something to wear that would allow for fair competition with Lisa.

Deion moved darkly through the evening streets. The moon was rising behind the skyscrapers of Yerba Buena's downtown. An area he had not been able to visit since he was an adolescent, since the riots of 2020. The light level of the nighttime city gradually rose as one moved towards the Bay Bridge. More windows emanated light and warmth from the families inside. In addition, the profusion of huge color LCD billboards harangued the inhabitants to purchase everything from tofu to tobacco. The occasional gasoline powered auto could be heard from time to time. However, most people moved around on foot or in the almost silent electric cars and buses. It would have been a nice night for a stroll were it not for the three figures that had been tracking Deion since he left the Mart.

Certainly, he had been followed before. Rival gangs often kept an eye on their competitors, but usually the lower-level grunts did the fighting and the dying. The problem tonight was that Deion could tell that he was being trailed by amateurs. One could only hope that everyone remained law-abiding: Deion actually disdained violence and tried to resolve conflicts through other means when possible. Unfortunately, at Bryant and 2nd the shadowy followers moved in for the kill. One ran forward, pulling a stun-baton as he moved. A second brought out a pulse-rifle and trained it on the prey, and the third, whom Deion deduced was a woman due to size and body language, took up a triangulated position with a silvery old revolver in her hand.

There are many schools of thought concerning whether a gun or a blade was best for hand-to-hand street combat. Due to an inability to jam, run out of ammunition, or misfire, Deion's first move was to draw a wickedly sharp six inch bowie knife. The baton whistled at his head, its electric charge crackling in the night and giving off a ghostlike blue nimbus. Duck, pivot, strike, withdraw, pivot, and Deion stood with a dripping blade besides a crumpled corpse.

The assailant with the pulse-rifle squared up to fire, but an amazingly fast moving flash of bright orange power ripped into the man and blew him halfway across the street. The woman swiveled, and got off one loud .45 shot before she too was blasted in half. Deion bent over his victim and began to search his pockets and body. After a moment, Chang, Deion's bodyguard appeared out of the shadows. The muzzle of his pulse-rifle still glowed orange in the darkness.

"Nice moves boss. I hope I didn't cut that too close?"

Deion looked up at Chang who was an extremely thin Asian of Chinese descent, with the same virus-enhanced black skin as his employer. Despite delicate features, Chang was an excellent shot. "All I care about is results." Deion looked back down to the body below him. "This guy was a nobody. No gang colors, tattoos, or haircut."

"Maybe they just picked on the wrong guy. The dude over here had a pretty lame weapon. It is one of those cheap local models with a weak electromagnet bottle. The thing is as liable to blow you up as nail the target." Chang was already slipping his top of the line PRC-made rifle back into his long-coat.

"Maybe you should call the consumer protection agency." Both men laughed as Deion stood up and began walking towards Market Street. Chang faded back into the shadows.

A few blocks later, they were back on their home turf. Deion slipped into an old commercial building on Mission

Street where he quickly moved through a raft of electronic and human security to enter a large circular conference room. There, eight similarly dressed and skin colored men waited quietly at an old, beaten up board table. This was the center of power of 'The Nights', the most powerful gang in San Francisco. Their boss put his briefcase down, and opened it to reveal hundreds of rows of carefully packed pill holders. Each holder contained ten shiny black caplets stamped in white with a letter "o". The drug had a different name in most countries, but in San Francisco it was known as Onyx.

"O.k. boys. Get it while it's hot. Let's get this stuff out on the streets" Each of the local dealers picked up 1,000 caplets and left quickly. Within half an hour the new batch of Onyx was on sale in all the major neighborhoods of the city. Within an hour certain unscrupulous Marines had been bribed and the drug entered Yerba Buena as well.

Vishali finished applying her makeup and ordered a solocab through her wrist-computer. After deciding on a pair of black pumps, she grabbed her purse and left the apartment. The elevator, signaled by the opening of Vishali's apartment door, was waiting and quickly delivered its charge to the ground floor where the cab was waiting.

The single seat vehicle, painted a bright yellow had a steering wheel, accelerator and brake pedals for those who preferred manual control, but Vishali simply clicked her tongue and asked to be taken to The Dive. The computer in the solo-cab immediately queried its database and its Global Positioning System before moving off towards downtown. An internal vehicle radar system and reception of telemetry from other moving autos in the vicinity insured an impact-free ride. Vishali relaxed and surfed through music videos on the net until the cab pulled up in front of The Dive at the end of Montgomery Street. Market Street, and The Fortified Zone loomed only a few feet away.

Vishali paid her fare by running a value card through the cab's reader and hopped out when the door was opened for her by The Dive's 300-lb. doorman/bouncer. After walking through a quick security scan, and paying a nominal $20,000 cover charge, she walked through the bar's large double-door entrance and followed a set of stairs down into darkness.

The strong THUMP-THUMP-THUMP-THUMP of a bass beat reverberated strongly through Vishali's sternum. Two stories down she entered the main room which had at one time been the storage level for a great office building that towered above her head. On stage, a four-man band was jamming, and across the room a huge video screen showed swirling psychedelic patterns. Two long bars lined the walls and swarms of patrons moved back and forth, dancing, drinking, smoking, flirting and snorting. A fluorescent black light glowed from panels in the walls, and red lasers danced down from the ceiling illuminating the avatar-figures of patrons visiting the bar from the cybernet.

A slightly translucent avatar took one look at Vishali's red miniskirt and moved towards her smiling: he was tan, tall, athletic and good looking. Vishali did not like dealing with these astral bar-hoppers. The real person behind the projected image could as easily have been a pimply-faced teenager, a retiree, or a woman as the tennis-pro lookalike before her. In addition, even if the cute guy were for real, he was as likely to be living in Sydney as San Fran.

"You look great," he yelled over the music by way of a first line. Vishali walked right through him - clearly the best way to blow off an unwanted avatar advance. She caught sight of her friends at the end of the bar furthest from the band. After trading cheek pecks with her four best friends - Lisa, Jim, Jasmine and David - she was introduced to Amir, one of David's co-workers. In less than a moment Vishali was

155

handed a glass of micro-brew wheat beer and was feeling at home despite the crush of bodies, booming music, and flashing lights.

Amir was obviously invited to be set up with the recently-single again Vishali, who, after an initial surge of anger and embarrassment over the situation decided to relax and check out the merchandise. Amir was a dark Israeli in his late 20s to early 30s with a confident demeanor, and quick, precise movements.

"So, are you another programming geek like Dave?"

"No," he replied. "I'm the financial funding manager for Quicken Bank. Not much of a job, I just make sure we have enough money at the end of the day." Vishali was impressed but tried to hide it. Intuit's Quicken Bank was one of the world's largest financial institutions due to its huge retail banking operation. Amir looked much too young for such a level of responsibility.

"So how did you meet Dave?"

"Oh, we do drugs together," Amir replied with a straight face. To prove his statement's veracity he quickly produced a shrink-wrapped strip of ten shiny caplets. Everyone in the group immediately focused on the pills as if Amir had just opened a big present at his tenth birthday party. "Onyx," he said with a wide grin. "Only the best for my friends". Dave reached out and placed the first pill in his mouth. Lisa, Jim and Veronica followed. Vishali hesitated for a moment.

"Ah...I haven't had this stuff before."

"It's the best Vish. Go for it," urged Lisa as she moved onto the dance floor.

"What is it?"

"It's a dual time-release smart virus," answered Amir. "The first one goes active immediately, squeezes right through the

156

blood-brain barrier, finds a home on your synapses, and...party time."

"And the second virus?"

"Oh yeah, it goes active five hours later and takes out the first virus." Amir popped another black pill while he was talking. Vishali noticed that Lisa's eyes were starting to glaze over as she moved her body in synch with Jim's on the dance floor.

"Why are you taking two?"

"Well, after awhile your natural antibodies get up the gusto to take on almost any virus, even a genetically engineered one, and then you've got natural resistance. At this point I need to kind of overwhelm my immune system"

"What if you build up resistance to the second virus first?"

"Well," Amir laughed. "I guess I might never come down from my high. That would be just terrible." He held a black caplet in the palm of his hand. "Put it in your mouth. Don't swallow it. Technology will do the rest."

Vishali screwed up her courage and popped the pill. The salivase in her mouth instantly dissolved the outer coating that had seemed so hard a moment before, and a pleasant-tasting powder spread across her tongue. Amir held up his hand. "Wanna dance?"

She followed him onto the floor, walking through a couple of slam-dancing avatars and saw that Lisa's face, now feverish, framed by a huge grin and dilated eyes. A wave of warmth passed over Vishali, and a moment later her expression matched that of her friend.

Chang moved to the front door of a garish 1970s cement block apartment building. After mumbling to the security computer, the door opened and he stepped inside to check that the entry area was clear. Then, returning to the entrance he stood silently and listened with his head cocked to one side. The street was empty and quiet, as it usually was at 3:00 am. After a moment he made a quick signal with his hand. Deion moved out of the shadows, went through the front door, ignored the elevator, and climbed the two flights of stairs to his apartment. Most hunted men avoid elevators when possible. Chang followed at a discrete distance and took up a position on the second floor landing.

At the metal security door, Deion spoke two voice authenticated password commands, and after hearing bolts slide back, produced an obsolete steel key and turned it inside an obsolete steel lock. He opened the door, closed it, ordered the computer to turn on the lights and relaxed. The cold metal of a gun barrel pushed into the back of his neck.

"Drop the gun. Drop the knife." Deion recognized the voice. It was Roxanne. "Drop your pants."

Deion did as he was told and stood motionless, but tensed as Roxanne walked around to face him. She held a huge automatic that seemed much too big for her. Most men would have been unable to resist staring down the barrel, at least for a second. But Deion never lost lock on her eyes. She reached into her tunic and pulled out a knife. It thumped as it hit the floor. Her gun followed. The tunic and the pants made less noise. Smart virus assisted or not, she looked good. Deion cleared his throat as he strode forward.

"[click] Lights off."

Vishali awoke to the almost painful pulsing of her wristcomputer. It was 6:00am and time to go to work. She sat up in bed, rubbing her eyes.

"[click] Windows clear." The opaque glass suddenly let through brilliant sunlight. Vishali covered her eyes and tried to get her brain to work. After a moment much of the preceding night's activities came back to her: she had stayed at The Dive until 2:00am, then gone with the group to the Golden Gate Bridge, had a swig of champagne looking out at the lights of the bay and the city, and then called it a night. The memory of a kiss or two with Amir moved like a whisper through her mind. Luckily she had not woken up next to him.

The thought of calling in sick was considered, then discarded. Not only did she have a conference call at 8:30am, but she was not hung-over at all. Amir's magic pills worked as advertised.

"[click] Shower on. 29 degrees C." Vishali slipped out of bed, confirmed that she was nude, and jumped into the shower. After washing the smell of smoke out of her hair, she dried off and dressed for work. The solocab was waiting for her at the curb, and she scrolled through financial news on the dashboard LCD as she was driven to work.

A ten minute ride through moderate traffic brought her to 550 California Street: the Bank of America building. With the slide of a value card she got out, and the solocab rolled away to its next pick-up. As Vishali passed through the lobby, the beam of a retina reader mounted in the wall reached out and caught her left eye. She never broke stride and rode the elevator to the 27th floor.

The doors opened to reveal a marbled floor reception area with a great view of the Bay Bridge. A young man sat at the desk, and above him were the large interlocked gold letters "LIM: Lesotho Investment Management" - an international fund manager with more than 100 billion New Rand under management. To the right were the gilded doors of the subsidiary LIM Private Bank branch where high net worth individuals parked their assets and paid dearly to be told by someone in an expensive suit that they were doing the right thing. Two guards flanked the doors like gargoyles.

Vishali smiled at Matthew behind the counter and walked down the hallway to the asset management division where her smallish office was located. The flat 50-inch computer screen hung on the wall over her desk was blinking angrily with an insistent message-waiting indicator. Messages from Shanghai and Johannesburg always came in during the night and early morning, and while they could be accessed anytime via wristcomputer, Vishali insisted on not working while out of the office.

First things first. Close door, sit down, and clear throat.

"[click] Standard morning computer setup for Sing1. Authenticate." A red laser probed out to reach her retina and the screen exploded into several different active windows, each a different color.

Most of the incoming data concerned global market activity, new stock recommendations, and corporate earnings announcements. The intra-company e-mail messages were mostly unimportant, but two caught her eye. The first confirmed her 8:30am conference call. The second requested her presence with the Chief Investment Officer (her boss) at 2:00pm.

Scanning over the windows, Vishali saw that not that much had happened during the night. Toyota was opening a new auto plant in Ethiopia, Intel was rolling out a new line of artificial intelligence mainframes, and Chinese forces were reportedly launching a counter-offensive in Myanmar against the native insurgents closing in on Yangon.

Most of the next half hour was spent preparing for the conference call. Finally, Greg Brennan, the marketing manager for non-Asian equity funds, sauntered into the office.

"How ya doing?" he said enthusiastically by way of greeting. "You all ready?" Always a salesman.

"Ready and able," she replied.

"You got your script?"

"I'm always ready in advance. You know that Greg." Vishali was kind but firm. "[click] Download 5/15/25 marketing presentation to drive A." The computer whirred and chimed. "All set Greg," she said.

"All right then, let's go." Vishali followed Greg out of the office into a conference room where Marc Roy was already waiting patiently. Vishali and Marc smiled at each other. They had both been hired into the investment area at about the same time a few years back, promoted to Portfolio Manager on the same day, and had always gotten along well. While Vishali made a point of keeping a division between work and pleasure, she had always been intrigued by Marc's aristocratic Gallic looks.

"Hey Marc, we all set?" Greg asked in salesman-speak. Marc only nodded politely. The two Portfolio Managers sat down next to each other at the table as Greg turned to the computer.

"[click] Time?"

"8:29am," the computer answered in a neutral male voice.

"[click] Initialize presentation one and two," the salesman continued as he faced the room's LCD screen. "[click] Time?"

"8:30am."

"[click] Do we have any participants on-line?"

"There are currently 412 World Class Club access representatives in the auditorium at this time. Eight more are currently logging in."

161

"Wow. Great turnout," Greg said importantly to Vishali and Marc. "Let's go get 'em! [click] "Activate two way link." With this, a red laser lanced out from just under the LCD screen and bathed Greg in its glow. The screen itself showed a virtual auditorium with seats filled by hundreds of avatars. They were of every ethnic background and represented the best producing brokers, trust officers, private bankers and financial planners worldwide who sold LIM mutual funds to their clients. Then an avatar image of Greg appeared on the stage. The real Greg cleared his throat, as did his avatar.

"Good morning, afternoon or evening, wherever you may be. I am Greg Brennan, Vice President of Retail Sales for LIM, and thank you for joining us for our monthly World Class Club investment update. Today we have with us the Portfolio Managers of the LIM Recovering Markets Fund and the LIM American Hemispheres Fund. I will introduce them to you and then we can get started.

"Ms. Vishali Sing has been with us for five years now. She was hired directly out of Oxford University in England where she concentrated in computer programming and history. She has been the lead portfolio manager of the LIM Recovering Markets Fund since its inception more than a year ago. This fund has performed quite well and is now up more than 32% in the last twelve month period."

"Mr. Marc Roy joined the company three years ago from the corporate finance department of Silverman Satchel. Prior to joining our organization, he received an MBA from INSEAD in France, and was employed by Alcatel in its new operations division. The LIM American Hemispheres Fund has been out a bit more than a year, and is up more than 13% in the last twelve months."

So with that, the portfolio managers will speak for about ten minutes each and then, time permitting, we will take questions. Vishali..."

Vishali stepped into the laser's glow and Greg moved away. Her avatar appeared on the stage. She noticed the LCD now showed a count of 587 participants in small glowing numbers on the bottom of the screen. An ethereal teleprompter appeared before her in the laser's beam. It showed scrolling text downloaded from her computer, but was not visible in the LCD's rendering of the virtual auditorium.

"Thank you for your time," she began reading. "As you know, the Recovering Markets Fund invests to achieve capital appreciation in the equity markets of North America and Western Europe. While these nations have been wracked by both war and civil disturbance in recent years, we here at LIM believe that the same qualities of innovation, education, hard-work and entrepreneurship that made these countries the industrial leaders in the twentieth century are still intact.

Thus, we are finding excellent investment opportunities today at attractive valuations ranging from the biotech industries in the fortified zone around San Diego to the armaments factories in Frankfurt-on-Main to the massive wind farms in The Republic of Texas. Despite the preponderance of a global economy centered in the PRC and its protectorates in east Asia, it is expected that western economies will recover in the next decade and regain a portion of their former position on the world stage. This trend is one of the primary reasons that LIM maintains an investment office here among the cybernet providers and software developers in the Yerba Buena fortified zone..."

As Vishali continued reading from the teleprompter, she sighed and wished that on this beautiful sunny day she could be somewhere flying a kite, rather than talking to a bunch of idiots on the cybernet.

Deion awoke but did not open his eyes. There was someone next to him in bed. Then the memory of Roxanne ricocheted like a bullet, confirmed by a quick glance to the woman sleeping next to him in his bed. While breakfast was his top priority, due to the necessity of missing his standard 3:00am meal last night, improving his apartment's security was a close second. If Roxanne could get into the apartment, so could someone interested in causing a slightly less pleasant effect on its primary occupant.

Slipping noiselessly from his bed, Deion left the bedroom, closed the door behind him, and went into the kitchen where he began to root through the refrigerator. Settling on a bagel with lox and cream cheese, he settled down at the table and relaxed for a moment and surveyed his domain: It was a large two bedroom apartment with a grand view of the Bay Bridge, Treasure Island, and the ruins of Oakland beyond.

Very few people had real money in San Francisco now, but those who did could afford very nice living quarters. Most city residents with employment outside of the giant mid-ocean fish farms and the circuit board sweatshops of the Peninsula were involved with the sale or consumption of various illicit drugs, weapons, or software. Deion was quite happy being on the sales side of that equation. 'The Nights', His 100-man strong organization owed itself to the simple strategy patterned on its leader's study of the ancient Romans: demand allegiance, practice tolerance, but brutally crush all dissent no matter what the cost. While Yerba Buena billed itself as a center for knowledge-workers for the future, that did not mean that its poor sister city on the wrong side of the concrete barricade was completely devoid of educated residents.

Deion was born in Atlanta, Georgia in 2018, the first child of a father who was a janitor and a mother who worked as a secretary for the local school district. The home was a strict matriarchy where all six young Washingtons were impressed by the need to rise to a higher level than their parents. At least one of the offspring listened: By the time the family moved to San Francisco in 2028, Deion was scoring in the top decile of every standardized test put before him, and he in turn, was thrown into a city magnet program in the affluent neighborhood of Presidio Heights.

Five years of the best schooling yuppies could subsidize was cut short when the great wave of riots swept the nation in the aftermath of President Spear's assassination., Deion, blocked by a concrete barrier from attending school, with one parent killed and the other thrown out of work, had no option but to start hustling on the streets. As he climbed up the chain of command in a local drug distribution gang, he was given a choice by his mother: get a decent job or move out. Deion had only seen his family twice in the last two years.

At first, the police took on the drug gangs. However, they soon learned the error of their ways, and concentrated on holding together what goods and services the city could still manage to provide. Life in San Francisco was no picnic for the average working man, but hospitals, supermarkets, schools, banks and even libraries continued to exist. Unfortunately, they were all a pale reflection of their opposites in Yuerba Buena. Almost anyone able to come up with enough New Rand or Yuan to make a significant bribe to the US Marine Corps emigrated as soon as possible.

Finishing the bagel, Deion opened his first Diet Dr. Pepper of the day and strode through to his study. A recently made large hole in the wall lead to the back stairwell. He almost dropped his soda in shock. For a moment he was furiously angry with Roxanne. But then he let loose a hearty laugh. If a gal wants in that bad, he thought, you got to let her have her way.

There were no messages waiting for him on his wrist computer (a rare item on this side of the fortified zone), and he placed it back on the desk. It was unusual for Deion to wear the chrome bracelet outside as it made him too easy to track. He dressed quickly and walked back to the bedroom where Roxanne was just beginning to stir.

"Yo," he said brusquely. "You can let yourself out the way you came in. See you get that patched up." Roxanne smiled at him, and Deion turned away before she had a chance to see him grin as well. Picking up his weapons in the front room he addressed the computer

"[click] Open door." He strode into the hallway where Bullet, his impressively muscular daytime bodyguard was waiting. The door closed, and Deion could hear the bolts sliding home. A quick turn of a key, and it was time to make the rounds.

Vishali was reading the part of Motorola's annual report concerning test marketing of a new jaw-embedded global communicator when the Lotus Scheduler chimed to remind her that it was time to meet with the CIO. She picked up a smart-pad and stylus, and walked down the hall to the office whose plaque read, Mr. Pieter K. Botha, Chief Investment Officer, LIM Western Hemisphere.

"Is this a good time?" Vishali asked as she peeked in through the door to where her boss was sitting.

"It's...fine," he replied "please close the door." Vishali did so and sat down in a leather chair. Marc was already occupying the second chair. Botha was a large bald man of almost seventy five. Alzheimer's and coronaries ran in his family, but smart-viruses had come along to insure that he was still vigorous and quick. He had been with the company for close to fifteen years after a long career as the manager of trust operations at Standard Bank of South Africa in New York. Vishali looked up to him as a mentor, and she hoped that he had come to hold some level of respect for her abilities in the last few years.

"I have some bad news for you Ms. Sing. As you know, we have been carrying this office for some time now. Even after the collapse of the U.S. economy, we always expected that there would be a recovery and the assets would flow in. However, since the PRC nuked Taipei and announced the Second Greater Asian Co-Prosperity Sphere, most of the market returns, and thus almost all of the flow of funds have gone to the other side of the Pacific. This office has been a laggard for years now, and we here at LIM have come to the point where some rationalization needs to take place." Botha paused to let what he had said sink in. Marc would not meet Vishali's eyes.

"Thus, we will be combining the Recovering Markets Fund with the American Hemispheres Fund, and we will only be needing one portfolio manager. I have decided that Marc is to be that manager. I am truly sorry, but there is no room in the budget for your services in the future. I will ensure-"

"But," Vishali broke in, anger rising within her. "My investment performance is better than his. I have been at the company longer-"

"My decision is final," Botha tried not to raise his voice. "The company will provide for three months' severance as well as outplacement counseling." Vishali glared at her now former superior. There was a knock at the door, and a large uniformed man from company security opened it slightly. Botha waved him back out.

"Look, I know you are angry right now. I am willing to act as a reference for you. Why don't you call me tomorrow morning and we can mull over your opportunities. I am afraid to have to do this, but the guard will stay with you at your office while you clean out your personal effects."

Vishali popped out of her chair and stormed out. She found that her hands were shaking. The guard followed. How could they be so unfair?, she screamed to herself. No notice, no warning, and they had even picked that damned frog instead of me! Suddenly, through the wave of anger, a plan gelled in her mind and became the focus of her attention. She would not be leaving empty handed!

Vishali stopped at the entrance to her office, and wiping tears from her face, addressed the guard. "I am going to use the bathroom. I will be right back. All right?"

The guard, seeing no other choice in the matter, nodded his assent. Vishali walked quickly by him towards the bathroom, but after turning the corner, ducked into Marc's empty office. She crouched down behind the desk. "[click] Computer, Log in for Sing 1. Authenticate. "The laser reached out, read her retina print, checked her voice against records and replied.

"Authenticated."

"Manual input and output only. New active window at grid D4." She grabbed the wireless keyboard off the desk and looked at the small screen that had opened upon her command. At the blinking cursor she typed:

ACCESS DIVIDEND DISTRIBUTION APPLICATION LIM 1724. This was the first project Vishali had been assigned to as a computer programmer hired fresh out of University.

ENTER ACCESS CODE. The computer replied in text.

HELLER 1416. The name of her superior on the project. The first name was Roger, and he had also been her lover before ending his life for reasons still unclear to Vishali. While her password access for the dividend program had long since been deleted, why would anyone remember to close out a dead man's. She quickly covered her eyes as the laser passed over her head

PLEASE SUPPLY RETINA ACCESS AND VOICE SAMPLE FOR AUTHENTICATION, the computer replied

OVERRIDE ICONA. The acronym stood for In Case of Nuclear Attack. Roger had programmed this into the initial software architecture so that the system could be accessed at a location where a retina scan was not available due to war, natural disaster, or other emergency.

OVERRIDE ACCEPTED

INITIATE CAPITAL GAIN DIVIDEND

WHICH MUTUAL FUNDS?

ALL MUTUAL FUNDS

SHAREHOLDER ACCOUNTS TO RECEIVE DIVIDEND?

PENSION ACCOUNT SING44-632-8789

PERCENT DIVIDEND OF NET ASSET VALUE?

99% (Vishali did not want accounts crashing all across the LIM system due to suddenly having zero balances)

There was a moment of silence.

DIVIDEND COMPLETE

Vishali grabbed a thumb drive out of a disk holder on the desk and shoved it into the drive slot.

TRANSFER ALL PROCEEDS OF SING44-632-8789 TO THIS TERMINAL DRIVE A

COMMAND WILL OVERWRITE ALL CURRENT DATA ON DISK. DO YOU WISH TO CONTINUE Y/N?

Y

PROCESSING

The indicator above the disk drive lit to show that it was active, and Vishali relaxed, surprisingly calm.

Inside the guts of the machine, billions of 1s and 0s were being downloaded onto the disk. But these were not just ordinary 1s and 0s: these strings of data added up to what most of the world used for money. Each year when governments wished to issue new currency they sent a list of serial numbers for the 'bills' to the Bank of International Settlements, or BIS in Basel, Switzerland. As the central bank for central banks, programmers placed three encryption codes before and after these serial numbers which identified the currency's nationality and face value. The encryption codes came from six different software companies whose composition was a secret and changed every few years. A final set of code inserted into the serial number acted as its own program and forced a rearrangement of the pattern of the encryption codes each time the serial number was accessed, scanned or transferred. Once a certain pattern had been used for a certain serial number, it could not be used again. This, plus six different encryption technologies prevented copying, thus making counterfeiting massively difficult.

With six codes to be arranged, and thus $6! = 720$ possibilities, each currency unit could be transferred 719 times, before the current holder was informed through a warning message that the unit needed to be transferred back to BIS for a replacement. Failure to do so resulted in the BIS software scrambling itself and the embedded serial number so as to render the currency unreadable and useless. The advantages over traditional paper money included the ability to move large sums at high speeds around the world with security. But like paper money, cybercash offered complete anonymity in transactions.

The red disk drive light turned off, MEMORY FULL. INSERT ADDITIONAL MEMORY TO COMPLETE COMMAND

Vishali grabbed another thumb drive out of the holder, put it into the slot, and shoved the first one into her suit pocket.

COMPLETE COMMAND

COMMAND WILL OVERWRITE ALL CURRENT DATA ON DISK. DO YOU WISH TO CONTINUE Y/N?

Y, Vishali slammed the letter home with exasperation.

PROCESSING

Vishali began to relax again, but suddenly the red light went off again. SYSTEM INTRUDER ALERT PROGRAM ACTIVATED. HELLER 1416 ACCOUNT LOCKED OUT. SING44-632-8789 ACCOUNT LOCKED OUT. SING 1 LOCKED OUT

Vishali was up and running. Suddenly she was scared. Marc walked right into her at the office door, and they both barely avoided falling to the floor. Vishali caught his eyes for a moment and saw he was puzzled. Then she passed him and headed for the elevators. As she turned the corner she saw the guard knocking on the door of the women's room. Vishali ducked back around the corner and hit the stairs. It was 27 flights down, and she was dizzy and sweating heavily by the time she reached the street. The brisk, dry air felt good on her face.

His Royal Majesty John Letumbu Mambazka walked the palace hallways. Despite the hour of 1:00am, he was wide awake. The Prince of Lesotho was not the first monarch in history to suffer from insomnia. All heads of state have concerns, but he arguably had more than most. The stout old man reached a balcony, rested his hands and absorbed the view. The Principality's capital of Maseru spread out below with most of its half a million inhabitants in the soft arms of sleep.

Unfortunately the city, which should have been in the center of the nation's 12,000 land-locked square miles, instead bordered the all-encompassing South Africa. Millions of squatter shacks leaned unsteadily on the other side of the guarded border. Their impoverished residents waiting for the morning's light to take them back to their daytime employment in Lesotho's diamond mines.

Maseru was intentionally sited close to the border and thus easily accessible to armed intervention by the old Apartheids when they first carved the 'tribal homeland' out of South Africa's vastness. One would imagine that a different chunk of land would have been chosen had there been knowledge then of the great veins of diamond coursing just a mile beneath the surface. Even now, the Union's government in Pretoria eyed Lesotho independence warily and insisted through back channels that the capital not be moved to a more central location nor the armed forces increased in size. A pliant attitude and a willingness to do certain 'favors' for its larger neighbor had insured independence to date.

Mambazka heard the sound of running footsteps coming towards him. His hand went to the ceremonial but serviceable Assegai spear at his side. But instead of an assassin, Buthelezi, his Prime Minister, slid to a stop and bowed.

"Your highness," he said between gasps for air. "We have a problem."

"When have we not?" replied the King.

"An immediate problem," the grizzled politician replied. "It seems that an employee of LIM in San Francisco hacked her way through our computer system and has made off with most of the assets in the mutual fund complex."

"She?"

"Yes, your highness. A 26 year old portfolio manager named Vishali Sing. But it is not who she is but what she took that is important: More than 30 billion New Rand!"

"Can we cover it?" the King asked with growing discomfort.

"The sum represents more than twenty times the equity of LIM. However, that and the sale of one of the larger diamond mines might be enough."

"What?" the King roared. He had become inured to the expectation of a stiletto between the ribs, but not an embarrassment of this magnitude. "Those mines are the sovereign property of Lesotho. They are not to be sold!"

"Yes your majesty. There is a chance that the funds can be recovered. Ms. Sing has only just absconded on foot with the funds. There are nine armed guards at the San Francisco LIM location. They have already been sent out to attempt to retrieve the disk."

"Make sure they are ordered to shoot to kill," the King pronounced with anger.

"My lord," Buthelezi said with a bow.

Vishali walked down California Street, the great ferry building rising at its end, quaint cable cars rumbling by on ancient machinery. Her mind was a rush: what to do, where to go. Yerba Buena was not going to be safe for long. She could head to the airport and fly to London where she had friends and family. That was probably best. She could catch a hydrofoil ferry to the Marin Headlands International Airport and pay for a flight, in cash. She certainly had the money. The ferry building was now only a few blocks away.

As she walked down the hill, Vishali heard the sound of a woman yell and a man swear. She turned to look and saw five security guards running towards her with pistols drawn. In the lead was the guard whom Vishali had given the slip. He did not look happy. A man and a woman had been pushed down as the guards ran by them.

Vishali started to run.

For the first time in her adult life, she felt pure panic.

A shot rang out and Vishali heard a guard yell to her "Stop! Stop now! She looked back and noticed a big quadcab motoring towards her. The occupants were LIM guards. She turned around. There was no way she was going to make it to the ferry building. As she got to the corner of Davis Street she noticed a solocab just to the right of her disgorging its passenger. Vishali dove in, took over the manual controls and floored the accelerator.

"Would you like some directions for the most time-efficient route to your destination?" The cab computer asked. Vishali did not answer. Davis dead ended into the concrete barriers and barbed wire fences of the Market Street at the border of The Fortified Zone. Directly in front of her was a sturdy looking gate and a lone Marine sentry facing away from her. A quick glance in the rear view mirror confirmed that the quadcab was gaining.

"All right," she thought to herself. "I'm going to San Francisco." She ripped the rear-view mirror off the windshield and shoved it under the brake pedal. Then she slammed on the accelerator. As the gate loomed closer, the cab computer calculated with its radar that an immediate stop was required to avoid a collision. It attempted to apply the brakes, but the rear view mirror prevented the movement of the appropriate pedal. Vishali fought the computer for control of the wheel, and won. The Marine, obviously shocked that someone was coming at him from the Yerba Buena side, barely moved out of the way in time.

Although the gate was solidly made the cab was able to punch through it. The windshield cracked, and Vishali was thrown forward, but the cab kept going. Suddenly she remembered that the Fortified Zone was protected by mines. She tried to hit the brake, but of course the rear-view mirror was still there. The door opened under her hand and she jumped, rolling across the pavement. The cab blew up even before she came to a stop. Luckily for her, the Claymore was aimed south, towards San Francisco, so most of the explosion and ensuing shrapnel was focused away from her.

The Marine yelled at her, and then turned just in time to have the quadcab pass him. Vishali got up and started to run toward the burning solocab. The Marine aimed his pulse-rifle at the quadcab, but was shot down from behind by the rest of the LIM guards as they arrived at the gate. The guards pulled to a halt, and all nine ran together past the burning frame in hunt of their prey. The Marines opened fire. Two LIM guards went down, cut in half by pulse-rifle blasts, but the rest kept going and were able to follow Vishali around the corner.

Vishali turned onto Mission and saw three large men standing in the middle of the street. They were had black-on-black skin and wore black from head to toe. She ran up to the largest, most muscular of them, completely winded, and grabbed him.

"Help! Help me!" she panted.

The men in black were pulling out weapons. She tried to hide behind the big guy. Suddenly there was gunfire. Then there was a great weight on her, bearing her down. The back of her head was the first thing to hit the pavement.

Darkness.

Deion had looked up while speaking to Jose, one of his best street dealers, to see a woman running towards him. She was of Pakistani or Indian descent, and quite beautiful. Her tailored business suit was out of place in the neighborhood, as was the pack of angry rent-a-cops chasing her. She ran up to Bullet, grabbed him and hid behind his bulk. Deion went for his gun. The rent-a-cops meant business. Bullet was trying to get his pulse-rifle out from under his coat when three slugs slammed into him. Deion dove behind a dumpster and came up firing.

Bullet had been a good bodyguard, and Deion was pissed. He emptied the entire magazine before ducking back for cover and saw one of the rent-a-cops go down. Bullets pinged off the metal dumpster as he reloaded. Across the street Jose had unlimbered his pulse-rifle and glanced over at Deion from behind the corner of a building.

So, five or six against two. Not the greatest odds, thought Deion. However, Jose was talking to someone on his wrist computer, and one could only hope that he was calling out the cavalry. Deion squeezed off a couple of blind shots to gain some time, and was rewarded by a rain of clangs as the dumpster stopped some more bullets.

A new round of firing, and footsteps as well. They were charging his position! Deion ducked his head out from behind the other side of the dumpster to see three rent-a-cops charging towards him. Their friends were firing at his position to keep him pinned down. Luckily, that is when Jose opened up with his pulse-rifle.

There were lots of reasons not to carry a new-fangled pulse-rifle: They were heavier than any traditional rifle, much more expensive, and no one had been able to miniaturize the system yet to produce a handgun model. However, there was one real advantage to the pulse-rifle: raw hitting power. When clicking off the safety, an electromagnet bottle formed just above the magazine power cell. Pulling the trigger released a stream of plasma from the magazine into the bottle which was then accelerated down the barrel at close to the speed of sound.

The resulting destructive force released was something that could reasonably be expected to blow a hole through four inches of carbon steel. In close quarters fighting this force was a significant advantage. Someone unfortunate to be hit by a bullet in the arm might still be able to pull a trigger to fire back. Someone hit in the arm by a pulse-rifle no longer had an arm.

Jose's first shot cut clean through two rent-a-cops. Their companion dropped prone to the ground but was blown away before he could take aim. The last three rent-a-cops turned their attentions to Jose as he ducked back behind his corner. Unfortunately for them, this gave Deion a chance to open up with his pistol. He blew the top of the head off one and the remaining two guards ducked behind the cover of a trash can and a building corner. The problem with taking cover in a fire fight against a foe packing a pulse-rifle is that there is rarely five inches of steel plate around when you need it. Jose blasted the trash can and the man behind it twenty meters down the street. The last rent-a-cop started running. Jose looked over at Deion who shook his head. Better to let one get away to spread the word that messing with this territory was a bad idea.

The two men walked into the middle of the body-littered street. Three minutes was more than enough time to create such carnage.

"What the hell was that all about?"

"Not us," replied Deion. "It was all about her." He pointed to the Indian woman pinned under Bullet's corpse. They rolled the hulk off, and Deion felt for a pulse: it was strong.

"I think she knocked her head when Bullet landed on her. Let's get her back to the office.

They carried Vishali deeper into San Francisco.

The Inkatha Airlines Boeing 6000 backed away from its gate at Durban International Airport right on time at 5:30am. The plane's 400 passengers were a mixed lot of businesspeople and tourists, blacks and whites and Asians on their way to Yerba Buena. Very few even took the time to look out the windows as the wings tilted, the jets fired down scorching the tarmac, and the craft took off, rising vertically to reach cruising altitude of 70,000 feet.

"This is IA 444 requesting permission to conform to standard northwest flight path Alpha Alpha.

"Roger IA, proceed," replied Durban air traffic control. "We are handing you off to Bloemfontein."

The plane's wings tilted to a horizontal position once again and the roar of the jets increased in intensity. IA 444 shot forward, broke the sound barrier and was soon moving at Mach 4.

At Bloemfontein International Airport in Natal, Louis Springbok was at work in the holosphere of the air traffic control room. He stood as a giant surrounded by the vast rolling plain of southern Africa with the cities of Durban, Maseru and Bloemfontein laid out at his feet like a set of children's toys. Glittering green lights at eye level represented moving aircraft, and next to each floated a readout indicating carrier, nationality, call letters and vector. Red lines lanced out from each aircraft indicating flight path to be taken, and blue lines showed what had already been flown.

It was a quiet morning, though it would get busier when a flock of flights from Asia and Europe started to arrive after 8:00am. Louis did not know why he looked over at IA 444 when he did, but somehow when you follow the planes long enough you know when something is wrong. Suddenly the green light representing more than 400 lives blinked out in a haze of static.

The pilot of IA 444 was daydreaming about surfing on the beaches of Natal when all his telemetry systems went dead. As planes mostly flew themselves these days thanks to fuzzy logic neural networks, losing one's computer guidance was a real problem. He and the copilot tried the radio, but to no avail. Then the head steward called in through the intercom saying that everyone using wristcomputers in communication mode had lost signal. That is when the pilot realized he was being jammed. It was also when he saw the two dart-shaped fighter jets with Lesotho military markings clear the cloudbank below him and take up positions on either wing.

A third dart took up a position ahead of the Boeing and waggled his wings, the universal aircraft signal for 'follow me'. The pilot had no choice but to obey. Out of the corner of his eye he noticed another Boeing with IA markings on what was supposed to be his flight path.

Louis was about to activate the downed plane alert when IA 444 appeared back in the holosphere, right where it was supposed to be. The telemetry signal was strong, and the red and blue flight path lines lanced back out to either side of the virtual projection area. He walked over and touched the green image of the plane to activate the communication system.

"IA 444. What is your status?"

"Bloemfontein control, our status is optimal. Unlimited visibility, low headwinds, and no weather in sight."

"We lost you down here a moment ago. Have you experienced any loss of telemetry or anything that resembled military jamming?"

"Jamming? Is everything all right down there?"

"Yeah. Continue on your flight plan. Bloemfontein out." The glinting green light of IA 444 passed over Louis' head and continued to the edge of his coverage area as the plane flew into Namibian airspace. Then it was gone along with its trailing blue line.

The real IA 444 landed on a dirt strip in the middle of a remote Lesotho airbase. Soldiers and armored vehicles surrounded the plane. A soldier walked in front of the plane and set up an amazingly low-tech hand lettered sign which read, "Do not be alarmed. Do not attempt to leave the plane. You will be allowed to resume your planned journey and jamming will cease in twelve hour's time."

The second Boeing 6000 reached the Atlantic Ocean and continued at six times the speed of sound towards San Francisco.

Vishali awoke disoriented, scared and harboring the echoes of a headache. As her eyes focused, the first impression was of being at a Halloween party. The room's walls, windows, furniture and inhabitants were black. Black-light bulbs provided illumination and forced teeth and eyes to glow brightly in what appeared to be their own incandescence. There was pressure on her arm, and in place of her wristcomputer, there was a Panasonic automedic.

"Hey, she's up," called out a teenager, carrying an ancient and monstrous AK-47 over his shoulder. The five older men sitting or standing around a conference table turned their attention to the couch and its occupant, and Vishali felt even more scared than she had before. One of the men, whom she had seen earlier on the street, walked towards her and smiled. He made a gesture, and everyone else in the room exited. His carriage implied confidence, intelligence, and she assumed, power.

"Nice of you to join us. We wanted to wake you hours ago but the doc there," he pointed to the device on her arm, "recommended against it. I'm Deion Sanders Washington, and I run things around here. What can we do for you?"

"Where," Vishali's voice faltered and she had to clear her throat. "Where am I, exactly, and where is my wristcomputer?"

"Well you see, you are my guest here in the lovely tourist destination of San Francisco. I imagine you remember how you came to enter our fair city?" Vishali nodded. "Good," he continued. "Well this is the headquarters building for my organization and wristcomputers have the unfortunate tendency to allow people to track down their owners. I'm sure you will understand why we had to destroy the instrument?" His voice was controlled, and reassuring.

"Yeah, well I can buy another one. Ah...are there any ferries to the Headlands' airport from here?"

Deion laughed heartily and exchanged a smile with the thin man who was also laughing. "I'm sorry my dear, but Marin Headlands International is part of the Yerba Buena Fortified Zone as I'm sure you know, and they don't allow in ignorant scum like ourselves. In addition, Ms. Singh, you've obviously been a very naughty girl, and it seems that there is a warrant out on your head for the charge of Theft of Proprietary Corporate Information."

Vishali blushed in anger. She was a professional, and no one spoke to her like that! Her anger was mixed with another emotion though. Just as quickly as the fear had left it was back again. Composing herself, she rose to her feet and looked Deion right in the eye.

"Look, I'm no girl, and I want out of this place before the police show up!" Her statement certainly did not have the intended result because Deion and the thin man started laughing again, this time even louder than before.

"I'm sorry ma'am," he replied, putting his hands up in front of him in a placating manner. "I won't call you a girl again, and we're not really laughing at you. You see, the police over here in San Fran don't like to come visiting so close to the Marines along the Zone that often. They tend to spring leaks when they do. Now about that company LIM that you stole something from, well they might be crazy enough to come a'knocking if it was like a special family heirloom or somethin'." At the mention of her company, Vishali unintentionally reached for the drive in her suit pocket. It wasn't there! Deion's eyes grew large. "So is that what they are after."

"Where is it? It belongs to me!"

"Oh, excuse me ma'am. You see, even around here it is unusual to see someone followed by a bunch of angry men firing guns. I thought that taking a look at the contents of that drive might give me a clue as to why. Not to mention why one of my best men is dead. However, it appears that the data is encrypted, and I imagine that both of us would be unhappy if my hackers accidentally scrambled its contents in an attempt to defeat its security."

"Look, Mr. Washington -"

"Deion, please."

"O.k. Deion. I am sorry about your friend's death. However, I must insist on your returning my property."

"Why should I?" he said with a grin.

Vishali was silent for a moment as she formed a reply. "You should return it because it does not belong to you and you seem like an honorable man, and secondly because I will be more than happy to reimburse you for your efforts."

Deion laughed, again and shook his head. "Ah, now you're talkin'." His eyes became hard. "What is on the disk Ms. Vishali Singh? Ms. Wanted for Theft of Proprietary Corporate Information?"

"Look, how much will it cost me to secure that disk's return?"

"How much is the information on the disk worth?"

Vishali closed her eyes. She realized that she was in way over her head. She was wanted by both the police and a powerful international corporation, and San Francisco, while not as bad as she had imagined it, was certainly not a safe place. "Look, I'll give you a third of what the disk is worth if you give it back, and if you can deliver me safely to London."

Deion laughed again. "This is like playing the old, Let's Make A Deal Show, from when I was a kid. London, huh? How do I know there ain't no donkey behind that curtain?" His eyes lost their mirth again. "Half."

"Fine. Half."

"So what is on the disk Ms. Singh?"

"30 billion New Rand."

Deion's face lit up and he laughed again as he stepped forward and put out his hand. "I sure do like that donkey Ms. Singh. I think we are going to like doing business together.

They shook hands. His grip was firm.

IA 444 decelerated to under 500 miles per hour and dropped its altitude as it entered the Bay Area. It passed over Point Reyes and turned south over the Pacific as it made its final approach for Marin Headlands International. At 9,000 feet the plane tilted its wings downward and fired its jets at maximum towards the sky. The aircraft actually broke the sound barrier as it rushed towards the ocean.

"Holy crap!" exclaimed air traffic controller Enrique Lopez as IA 444 suddenly disappeared from view in his holosphere. He and his colleague Lisa Benton exchanged a worried glance as a boom was heard through the walls of the control tower.

"Was that-"

"Get the look-down satellite on it now!" Benton snapped. Lopez pulled a remote control out of his pocket, and aimed it at the area where the missing plane had last been seen. As the telemetry from the satellite came in, the hologram area enlarged, and individual seagulls and waves could actually be discerned. But there was no plane, no wreckage, just empty ocean.

Colonel Yangi Zomba personally piloted IA 444 as it crossed back onto land over the trailer parks of Ocean Beach. He flew below 300 feet at 1,200 miles an hour, and his hands were sweating underneath leather gloves. As he passed Twin Peaks, the alarm of the proximity radar sounded, and its klaxon rattled him as he swung the plane between the hills and accelerated east. At the last moment, he rotated the wings almost completely around and opened up the throttle to slow the Boeing. After that, it was an easy matter of making a normal vertical descent to land in the derelict field that had once been the site of Candlestick Park.

Before the jet engines had even been shut down, the doors swung open and infantrymen of the Lesotho 2nd Division were fanning out to form a defensive perimeter. Several squatter families lived on the pothole-marked field, but the sight of large African soldiers carrying pulse-rifles, spears and grenade launchers made them skittish. A warning shot or two convinced them to leave - quickly. Zomba stepped onto the sodden field and solemnly touched the ground. One of his earliest memories was of waking up in the middle of the night after a bad dream and crawling into his father's arms while he and his friends watched a football game from San Francisco in the United States of America.

A long ramp descended from the rear of the plane and after a moment, vehicles began rolling down onto the muddy turf. Each was a military 4X4 with a non-descript coat of gray still drying over the savannah camouflage paint.

The contact, a tall man in a garish red leather suit, appeared at the south east gate bracketed by a fading 3COM sign. He was searched and then escorted to the Colonel by two Lesotho soldiers.

"I'm Donk. I know where the girl is," he mumbled.

"Where," demanded the Colonel.

"In the den of the bats my man, the den of the bats."

"Take us there."

That's what I get paid for," was the quiet reply.

Zomba waved his Assegai over his head. "Mount up Force One. Let's move!"

Soldiers scrambled into 4X4s and, under the eyes of a covering force of thirty remaining men, drove north for the center of the city.

"So what do you want to do with your money Ms. Singh?"

Vishali looked up from the corn chowder that had been politely supplied by one of the younger Nights along with some pain killers for her headache. Deion was looking over at her with an curious smile. "I'm not sure," She replied. "I guess I had always wanted to be rich, and now I will have my chance."

"But you're a Fortified Zone professional. Aren't you already rich?"

"Not really...just comfortable. My parents had to declare personal bankruptcy when I was in University. I almost had to drop out. I guess that scarred me a bit. Since then, I have been sending about half my wages back to the family, and I always wanted to get to the point where I would have real liquid wealth. Now I can have that chance, and maybe do something good for the world while I am at it. I just don't know what that good is yet."

"Very noble. Me, I never had a choice about becoming rich. It was either climb to the top of the pile here or get smothered underneath. But with my half of that drive's assets, I will be able to find a much larger pile on which to play king o'the mountain."

Vishali took another spoonful of soup and hesitated before asking her next question. "Deion, why are you not just taking the whole drive from me and forcing me to give you the access code?"

Deion laughed heartily. "Vishali," he began, using her given name for the first time. "I wondered how long it would take you to ask me that. I am impressed though that you had the cojones to ask me while sitting here in my little personal den o'iniquity. Believe me, I thought about it. But I decided it just wasn't right. You may not agree with me, but I do consider myself a businessman. I have never harmed anyone who did not try to harm me first. My 'Nights' don't steal, they don't cheat, they just sell goods and services at market clearing prices and help the economy to function... Someday I may wonder why I gave up the opportunity to have an extra 15 billion Rand, but that day ain't here yet. For now, you obviously need protection, and I am willing to sell it to you for a fairly agreed-upon price."

Vishali let out a quiet sigh of relief and dipped her spoon back into the soup while Deion spoke in hushed tones to one of his men who had just entered the room. She stole a glance at her host through her lashes. He was a cute one: buff, calm, poised, and very smooth.

He looked back at her and she stiffened. His eyes had become very hard. Then the sound of pulse-rifle fire erupted nearby and an explosion rocked the building. "It seems your friends are back, and this time they aren't playing so nice." The sound of the fighting raged closer, and Deion grabbed Vishali roughly by the hand. "Move it!" he yelled even though she was right next to him.

186

A couple of moments later and they were in the front seat of an old '99 Ford Mustang 5.0 facing a windowless garage door. Deion spoke through the open window to his men who were standing next to the car. "Don't try to hold them off after we get out of here. Just take the most valuable stuff you can carry, and get out through the emergency tunnels. Set up at the emergency HQ, and lay low for a couple of days. I'll see you soon." With that, he gunned the engine, and one of the men reached low and pulled the garage door up violently. The other four 'Nights' let loose with their pulse rifles even as the Mustang shot forward. Two Lesotho 4X4s set up in a roadblock position were blown backwards, and Deion screeched between them. Vishali looked up to see several soldiers turn towards her in surprise as they motored past. The sound of gunfire became intense as 'The Nights' in the building opened up with their weapons to cover their leader's escape. A massively hot blast from a Lesotho Special Forces pulse-rifle blew out the rear window, and then Deion pulled the car around a corner in a scream of burning rubber. Suddenly things were quiet again.

"Where are we going?" Vishali asked nervously.

"To the safest place around. We are going to pay the US Marine Corps a visit." Five minutes of high speed driving later they arrived in sight of a guardpost along the fortified zone where it reached the San Francisco Bay. Deion got out of the car with his hands in the air, and motioned for Vishali to follow. The two Marines who were visible eyed them wearily. A challenge rang out at twenty meters, when they reached the first low concrete barrier.

"Stop and state your purpose here!" The Marine speaking looked angry. Vishali could almost feel all the weapons that must be trained on her that very moment. Her knees were growing a bit weak. In contrast, Deion appeared totally calm as he replied.

"How much for passage on your next transport out of here."

"What?"

"How about 10 million Rand?" There was a long pause. "For each of us? No questions asked."

A Major appeared at the gate and motioned Deion and Vishali forward. Two marines patted down their two visitors and relieved Deion of his pistol and his knives. As they were led through the gate, a blast shook the ground as the Mustang erupted in flames.

"It seems that your friends have arrived." Deion said to Vishali. A few Lesotho 4X4s hove into view, but prudently backed off upon being confronted by the Fortified Zone, and its heavy weaponry.

The Marines were happy to provide Vishali with an e-commerce terminal to which she transferred 20 million Rand. After that they were quickly escorted to a hovercraft that took them out to the military airbase on what had originally been the central span of the Bay Bridge before the quake of '23 had dropped the portion closest San Francisco, along with 306 motorists, hundreds of feet to the waiting water below. Throughout the trip, the Marines were respectful, though they spent a good deal of time passing somewhat wary glances at Deion.

Once on the base, a particularly grizzled Marine approached the two refugees.

"So I hear that you are to be our passengers this afternoon. We have two transports leaving in the next hour. One to Seattle, the other to New York City."

"We'll take New York," replied Deion.

"Very good. Private, please escort these two to the appropriate craft. Make sure they make it on. I don't want them on my base any longer than necessary."

As they were walked across the tarmac Vishali asked, "Why New York?"

"I have some friends there," was his only reply.

The massive military cargo aircraft lifted off in less thn 30 minutes. Vishali was seated against a window with Deion next to her. In the jump seat across the aisle, a Marine kept a wary eye on them at all times. The San Francisco Bay spread out below them as the jet thrusters launched the plane skyward. Vishali gazed out the window at the downtown Yerba Buena where her office was/had been. It was a clear day, and she could also see clearly across to the massive red metallic structure of the Golden Gate Dam that kept out the ever-rising Pacific Ocean. Great pumps sucked the fresh water of the Bay over the top of the dam to the thirsty Chinese tankers on the other side. She lay back in the seat and slipped into an exhausted, and dreamless sleep.

Almost two hours later she awoke near to their destination. Vishali looked out of the window towards the aging metropolis of Manhattan. From far above, the great buildings rose up like needles pointing at the sky. In the moonlight, one could see the water glistening down the avenues and lighting up the myriad of gypsy boats on Central Park. The plane descended swiftly towards the sunken grave of the South Bronx and landed on the great floating platform which was the Al Sharpton Memorial International Airport. Another small bribe, and a bus was procured to take the two civilian passengers to the non-military terminal. Upon disembarking, Deion moved warily. He was nervous to be unarmed when protecting a fortune in stolen e-cash. However, all went smoothly, and a black skinned and clad man awaited them with an open smile on the far side of the flight security checkpoint.

"Good to see you Jesus," said Deion with a smile.

"Thank you for visiting our fine city. I hope that you will accept this gesture of our hospitality." A blunt-nosed gun passed between the two men and disappeared into Deion's jacket pocket.

"Vishali, this is Jesus. He is the second in command of the local chapter of my organization here in New York." Deion looked sideways at the man before continuing, "One would hope that he will be willing to assist us during our stay."

"I believe Mr. Washington is right," replied Jesus with a laugh as he placed an arm around Deion's shoulders. "I owe him big time."

"Why is that?" asked Vishali.

"Maybe it would be best if I tell you on our ride into the city. Come along, we have a limo waiting."

They proceeded outside, past a line of yellow cabs, and slipped into the black limousine that waited for them at the edge of the dock. The ship rode low and fast through the dark waters of the two-mile wide East River. Vishali leaned back in the plush seats and slowly allowed herself to relax. The two men reminisced over cold beers from the wet bar.

"Deion got us started out here. My older brother and I really pissed off the leader of the Red Hots-"

"Red Hots?" she asked.

"They are a rival organizations of mine in San Francisco," replied Deion. "You may have seen one of their members. They wear nothing but bright red leather." Vishali shook her head.

"Well anyway," Jesus jumped back in to his story. "This...gentleman was very angry with the two of us, and Deion here was kind enough to send us out here to the Big Apple with enough seed capital to stake a claim. I don't understand why you don't come out here yourself Deion. One doesn't have to deal with fortified zones here to sell product to the wealthy, just get yourself past the guard posts on the Jersey and Suffolk County shores and you're in. The best restaurants, the excitement"

"Oh, I'm happy in San Fran my friend."

190

The limo pulled out of the traffic of the FDR Waterway at 65th street and pulled up at a tall apartment building on the northwest corner of Third Avenue. A new entrance had been built into the fourth floor at the waterline. As Vishali got out of the limousine, Jesus pointed to the large open-air cafe built on what had once been the flat roofs of the old townhouses beneath their feet. "What do you say we have a drink?"

The three sat down at a table next to a large glowing coal brazier that warmed the night. Deion looked a bit wary.

"You know Jesus, I'm afraid that this is not all that good an idea. I really wanted to keep a low profile. There are some people looking for us, and they are pretty god dammed mad."

Jesus took a swallow of his beer and snorted before he answered. "This is my hood man. I've got a bodyguard keeping you covered right over there," he indicated a dark shadow over to the right. "Who is going to bother you around here?"

Deion slipped the ugly gray gun out of his pocket as he answered, "How about those guys." Several figures carrying pulse-rifles had suddenly appeared at the edge of light where Jesus' bodyguard had recently been standing. A lifeless form slumped forward into the edge of the light. Deion had just taken up a position behind the brazier when he felt the hard edge of a gun muzzle press up against the back of his head.

"Twice in two days!" he muttered to himself as he gently placed the gun on the ground. Five Lesotho troopers were standing around the table, and one pulled Deion to his feet while another took Jesus' gun out of his hand.

"You three have no time to mess around with me! Where is the money!" shouted Zomba.

Vishali was shaking as she pulled the drive out of her pocket. "It's all right here. Just don't kill us." Zomba reached forward to take the stick of plastic from her hand, but she did not like the look of fierce triumph in the African's eyes. With

191

a will she did not know she possessed, Vishali tossed the drive through the air in a short arc that landed in the heat of the coal brazier. The plastic melted almost instantly.

"That was a very, very stupid thing to do," Zomba said with controlled fury as he leveled his gun at the center of her chest.

Suddenly, three fast attack heliplanes roared overhead in a blaze of white light and a mist of spray was whipped off the fetid water of the Avenue. Scores of police in riot gear and carrying assault rifles appeared on all sides of the cafe, some emerging from the apartment building, and others arriving in fast attack boats.

"This is the New York City Police Department," an amplified voice boomed out. "You are covered on all sides, drop your weapons and lie down on the ground." All warily followed the order.

A cop cuffed Zomba's hands behind his back, and yelled into his ear. "We don't like people violating our airspace and coming into our city without permission to threaten our citizens with guns. Only we get to do that!"

As the Lesotho troops were led away, a burly policewoman searched Vishali, Deion and Jesus and looked over their ID's. "Are those your guns?" she asked pointing to the men's pistols on the ground.

"Oh no Sir," Deion replied. "Those nasty uniformed guys must have dropped them in all the excitement."

"Yeah right," she replied. "Well I don't know why those idiots were after you, but I don't want you West Coasters in my town come tomorrow evening. Understand?"

"Yes sir," Deion replied. And suddenly, they were gone: the police, the soldiers, and most of the other patrons of the cafe.

Deion turned to Vishali. "Ms. Singh, I don't really mind that you threw your money into the fire over there, but we've got

192

one small problem. You owe me 10 billion New Rand."
Jesus' eyes grew wide at that, and he looked towards the
brazier.

"Hmmm," she replied. I never said 10 billion New Rand,
Deion. I only agreed you could have half of what was on the
drive. In fact, I'll even let you have all of it now if you want
me to fish the thing out of the brazier." Deion grimaced and
his countenance showed the onset of anger. "But," Vishali
continued, "I am sure I can think of some way to repay you
for all your time." She reached up and kissed Deion hard on
the lips. After a very short second he returned the gesture.

His Royal Majesty John Letumbu Mambazka stood once
again at the railing looking out into the night. The theft in
San Francisco was a serious blow indeed, It insured that his
insomnia would take a strong hold this evening. From the
shadows, the slow measured pace of the Prime Minister
approached. Buthelezi bowed slowly in front of the monarch
before starting his report.

"Your highness. I am afraid that our men have been
unsuccessful in their endeavor to recover the stolen funds. In
fact, the matter has taken on an even more serious tone. Not
only were the stolen funds destroyed, but the majority of our
commandos were arrested in New York City. It is likely that
a formal protest will be issued to our ambassador in the
morning. Our bankers have heard rumors of our recent
problems and are interested in the immediate repayment of a
portion of their loans. As your Prime Minister, I would have
to recommend that we sell a portion of the ownership of one
of the two diamond mines."

The King pulled himself up to full height in outrage, "I will
not sell. It is the national heritage. There must be some other
way!"

"The Crown Prince agrees with me, you highness. We have little choice in the matter."

"I care little what my son thinks in this matter! I am still alive, and I will make decisions for the nation."

"As you wish." Buthelezi bowed slowly, lower and lower than the King had ever seen him bow before. That this was unusual did not occur to Mombazka until he suddenly heard a soft footfall behind him. He never saw the assassin. He only felt the bright pain as the knife slipped in between his ribs. The blade found the King's heart, and the monarch fell to the tile floor.

"The King is dead," murmured Buthelezi as he rose from the deep bow. "Long live the King."

A graduate of Harvard Business School and a former field agent for the Federal Reserve Bank of New York, the author spent more than 20 years running billions of dollars as a Portfolio Manager of both Mutual Funds and Hedge Funds in New York and San Francisco at firms ranging from Merrill Lynch, to AIM to Ascend Capital. Mr. Ellman resides in Tiburon, CA with his wife and sons.

The growth of the capital markets since the 1990s has handed enormous power to a handful of men and women answerable to no one except their investors. What happens when this power is used for personal greed and ambition? RISK CAPITAL takes you on a global ride from the cool glass towers of Manhattan to the steamy jungles of the Yucatan - from secret meetings in a mountain-top Swiss castle to the very depths of evil men's souls.

Praise for RISK CAPITAL

'Cross the Magellan Fund with James Bond and Gordon Gecko and you've got James Ellman's RISK CAPITAL'

Mike Yellen, Portfolio Manager, AIM Global Health Care Fund

'If it sells a million copies it will be a best seller.'

James Bogin, Founder, Legend Asset Management

'James Ellman is the early 21st Century's answer to Jonathan Swift'

Andrew Boczek, President and Chief Investment Officer, Gulliver Investments LLC

'Long at the top, short at the bottom'

Brian Urey, Emerging Markets Trader, Robert Fleming Securities